MODERN TRENDS IN HINDUISM

PHILIP H. ASHBY

COLUMBIA UNIVERSITY PRESS
NEW YORK AND LONDON 1974

Philip H. Ashby is William H. Danforth
Professor of Religion at Princeton University.

COPYRIGHT © 1974 COLUMBIA UNIVERSITY PRESS
PRINTED IN THE UNITED STATES OF AMERICA

LIBRARY OF CONGRESS CATALOGING IN PUBLICATION DATA

ASHBY, PHILIP H

MODERN TRENDS IN HINDUISM.

(LECTURES ON THE HISTORY OF RELIGIONS, NEW SER.,
NO. 10)

INCLUDES BIBLIOGRAPHICAL REFERENCES.

I. HINDUISM—HISTORY.   I.   TITLE.   II.   SERIES.

BL1150.A83   294.5'09   73-20262

ISBN 0-231-03768-6

FOR
JOAN, PHILIP, LLEWELYN,
AND
THEIR GENERATION IN INDIA WHO
WILL LIVE TO SEE THE HINDUISM
OF THE TWENTY-FIRST CENTURY

This volume is the tenth to be published in the series of Lectures on the History of Religions for which the American Council of Learned Societies, through its Committee on the History of Religions, assumed responsibility in 1936.

Under the program the Committee from time to time enlists the services of scholars to lecture in colleges, universities, and seminaries on topics in need of expert elucidation. Subsequently, when possible and appropriate, the Committee arranges for the publication of the lectures. Other volumes in the series are Martin P. Nilsson, *Greek Popular Religion* (1940), Henri Frankfort, *Ancient Egyptian Religion* (1948), Wing-tsit Chan, *Religious Trends in Modern China* (1953), Joachim Wach, *The Comparative Study of Religions,* edited by Joseph M. Kitagawa (1958), R. M. Grant, *Gnosticism and Early Christianity* (1959), Robert Lawson Slater, *World Religions and World Community* (1963), Joseph M. Kitagawa, *Religion in Japanese History* (1966), Joseph L. Blau, *Modern Varieties of Judaism* (1966), and Morton Smith, *Palestinian Parties and Politics That Shaped the Old Testament* (1971).

PREFACE

This book is the result of a series of lectures given in 1968–1969 under the auspices of the Committee on the History of Religions of the American Council of Learned Societies. In preparing the lectures and the subsequent book the author has been greatly aware of the variety in the composition of his audience. Undergraduates, teachers, scholars, and the general public were present at the lectures. Their response and their participation in the question periods that followed were of great aid in the preparation of this book. Most especially, I am grateful to the Hindu students and scholars who were present at many of the lectures in this country. They did not allow me to go unchallenged when they thought me to be in error in fact or interpretation. By their debate, their kindly suggestions, and their encouragement they played an important role in the presentation of contemporary Hinduism that follows.

I am particularly grateful to the chairman of the Committee, Professor Joseph L. Blau of Columbia University, for his role in arranging for the lectures and to my many hosts at the institutions where the lectures were given. The series of lectures was presented in whole or in part at the University of Chicago, Northwestern University, the Hartford Seminary Foundation, Colgate University, the University of Tennessee, Columbia University, Union Theological Seminary in New York City, the University of Pennsylvania, Harvard University, Southern Methodist University, and Duke University.

I am especially grateful to Princeton University for the granting of a McCosh Faculty Fellowship that enabled me to return to India for conversations and research during the academic year 1967–1968. My indebtedness to Indian friends and new acquaintances is immeasurable. Two friends of long standing, Khushwant Singh, the Indian novelist, historian of Sikhism, and present editor of the *Indian Illustrated Weekly,* and Professor K. Satchidananda Murty, head of the Department of Philosophy at Andhra University, were particularly helpful in their suggestions.

Professor N. Subba Reddy, head of the Department of Anthropology at Andhra University, was an invaluable counselor and guide in the structuring of the study of Hindu youth discussed in chapter III. Two young research scholars at the University, V. Arjanna in anthropology and T. Narasimha Moorthy in philosophy, were of great aid in interviewing the students and carrying out the many duties connected with the study.

The gracious courtesy of Satguru Charan Singh Ji Maharaj, the Master of the Rādhā Soāmī Satsaṅg discussed in chapter IV, continues to serve as the source of many pleasant memories. And the helpful hospitality of his faithful servant Śrī Dev Prakash contributed greatly in making the stay at Beas a delight long to be remembered.

The warm friendliness of the Indian people and their desire to help the foreign visitor to know them better was particularly evident in my reception by Śrī Gurujī Golwalkar of the Rāshtrīya Swayaṁsevak Saṅgh and Śrī K. R. Malkani, the editor of the weekly *Organiser.* Busy leaders took time to answer my questions with patience and courtesy.

Mrs. Denise Landry typed the manuscript in its final form and worried over the diacritical marks with her usual good humor. Ms. Karen Mitchell of the Columbia University Press made many helpful suggestions by her careful editing of the manuscript. My wife, accompanying me to India for the first time, found a people she had read about, and of whom I had talked about so often, to be all that she had envisaged them to be. In the midst of helping me in many ways she found a country of beauty and a warm and gracious people.

PRINCETON UNIVERSITY   PHILIP H. ASHBY

A NOTE CONCERNING PRONUNCIATION

A word needs to be said about the problem of pronunciation and the use of diacritical marks in this book. Anyone who writes what it is hoped will be of interest both to scholars and the general reader is confronted with numerous problems. In the instance of this book the scholar rightly should expect a scholarly transliteration of Sanskrit, Hindi and other Indian words. The general reader, on the other hand, may understandably be confused by diacritical marks and the absence of vowels.

The attempt has been made to strike a balance between the legitimate concerns of both types of readers. However, as long as some in the West continue to pronounce Ramanuja as Ramanewjaw or Atman as Utman it will be necessary to write Rāmānuja and Ātman.

In this connection a letter to the editor of the *New Delhi Statesman* by a pro-Hindi and anti-English language reader may be of interest to those of us born in the English-speaking world. He pointed to the difficulties of English pronunciation by claiming that "ghoti" should be pronounced "fish," since *gh* is *f* in "laugh" and "tough," *o* is *i* in "women," and *ti* is *sh* in "ration" and "nation."

For the general reader the following may be helpful. The long vowels *ā, ī, ū* are pronounced as the *a* in father, the *i* in machine, and the *u* in rule. *Ṛ* is pronounced as the *ri* in rich; *ś* or *ṣ* while slightly different from each other may generally be pronounced as the *sh* in ship, and *c* is pronounced as *ch* in chair.

CONTENTS

MODERN TRENDS IN HINDUISM

INTRODUCTION

Interest in India on the part of Western peoples has grown dramatically in the decades since the Second World War. Like the Asian world as a whole, India has always had an element of fascination and mystery for those who have read about it, and usually an even greater allurement for the foreigner who has visited it. The non-Indian who has lived a part of his life in the country and/or has been a serious student of its religion, culture, and society often discovers his enchantment and curiosity to be accompanied by a knowledge of India and its people that is not without an element of frustration. In some measure this bafflement is but a part of the usual, recognized problems accompanying the endeavor to understand something foreign. But those who have developed affection for the wonder that was and is India seldom escape the conviction that there is something different, something inexplicable, within the Indian ethos.

Knowledge about the world and its peoples has changed greatly since Strabo wrote about India in his *Geography* in the first century. Nevertheless, one cannot escape the feeling that what he said in his introduction continues to be true:

The reader must receive the account of this country with indulgence, for it lies at a very great distance, and few persons of our nation have seen it; those also who have visited it have seen only some portions of it; the greater part of what they relate is from report, and even what they saw, they became acquainted with . . . in great haste. . . . they frequently contradict each other.[1]

Obviously, today the distance to India has greatly decreased and the number of people who have seen more and more portions of it continues to increase at a rapid rate. Western youth, adult dilettantes, and people of all ages who are disillusioned with things Western are finding in Asian culture in general, and for some Indian culture in particular, answers they seek about themselves and the meaning of life. Some of these see and experience the home areas of the cultures that entrance them; others not as fortunate hear and read the claims of exponents both native and foreign. In either case, they are all too often possessors of limited knowledge and, unfortunately, are unaware of the limitation.

Many professional students of India hold the conviction that while portions of the variety that constitutes India may be seen and fairly well known, too often they are believed to be the whole when in fact they are only constituent and dependent parts. The well-intentioned Indian scholar or the enthusiastic exponent may well forget the variety of the tradition in which he has his grounding as he seeks to present that in which he has well-founded pride. This is understandable, and few interpreters of their native culture from any tradition escape this danger. And the non-native convert to a foreign mode of life and/or religious tradition is proverbially extreme in his enthusiasm and narrow in his exposure to, and understanding of, that which he now fervently espouses.

All this is particularly true of Western understanding of the Indian religious tradition and its major expression, Hinduism. The Western scholar is keenly aware that defining Hinduism is a complex and, perhaps, impossible problem. The layman usually believes that what he has learned is Hinduism and is unaware of the complexities that combine to create the total Hindu religious ethos. Or he is unconcerned about anything within Hinduism other than what he finds valuable, because his interest is primarily that of a

[1] *The Geography of Strabo*, trans. by H. C. Hamilton and W. Falconer (London, 1889), Vol. III, Book XV, chap. 1, vs. 2, p. 73.

religious seeker rather than a student of human thought and culture. The scholar can have little or no scholarly complaint with what the religious seeker finds worthwhile for himself; nevertheless, he cannot escape a sense of irritation with such a person's all too frequent confusion of what he or she finds personally valuable in the Indian religious atmosphere with the Hinduism of the vast majority of the Indian people.

Nor has the scholar escaped dangers in his own endeavors to understand Indian religion more fully and more accurately. Too often, the scholarly interest in other religions and cultures has been of a historical rather than a contemporary nature. Until recent years we historians of religion have been particularly guilty in this regard. We have either succumbed to the old and still present Western tendency to believe that nothing outside the Western world is of much value to the modernized, contemporary man or woman of the West; or we have thought of the world's non-Western cultures as being so lethargic, and perhaps decadent, that we have dismissed them on the assumption that today they do not even possess viability or vitality in their own homelands.

This situation is rapidly changing. Anthropologists, sociologists, historians of culture and religion, and others are reminding us that not only are non-Western cultures and religions alive and meaningful in the areas of their traditional influence, but perhaps they also have something to contribute to so-called modern man, whether he be Eastern or Western, scientifically oriented or traditional. Most importantly, we have become keenly aware that if we are to have even an elementary understanding of world culture and religion in the last decades of the twentieth century, it is essential that we be informed as to the conditions and currents of movement present in traditional cultures and their related religions today.

Our concern in this book is with *Modern Trends in Hinduism.* As the primary religious expression within Indian history and culture, Hinduism encompasses variety, marked differences, and subtle nuances. Some of this variety will be visible within our discussion; awareness of much of it and its critical importance in understanding

Hinduism will be limited to the reader who has a wider and deeper acquaintance with Hinduism than that furnished by this book.

There are three general principles that I would suggest as guides in our attempt to understand Hinduism as it is today, both as a factor in India itself and as a potential, if not already active, partner in religious cultural affairs beyond its traditional boundaries.

The first principle regards the interrelationship between separate religions with their traditional cultures and other religions and cultures. No attempts are being made today to import or borrow that which is foreign in order to displace what is indigenous and traditional. This may not be true in matters which fall in the category of technology, economics, or of political structure, but it must be recognized in the sphere of religion. We cannot understand modern trends in Hinduism without constantly reminding ourselves of this self-evident fact.

It is customary when one speaks of the Eastern areas of the world today to refer to the development of nationalism, to economic needs, plans, and developments, to educational requirements and attempts at their fulfillment, to a growing cultural self-awareness and its expression through various media, and to note in each category the impact of Western concepts and the influence of Western standards. Students of religion have done the same in their descriptions of the religions of the East, and in the past there was some justification for so doing. But there is also grave danger that in recognizing the importance of Western impact and Western criteria confusion will result and it will be assumed that the ultimate end of things will be a Westernization of that which is native to the East. The norms of religion, by subtle inference, come to be conceived of as residing in the West and its religious beliefs, traditions, and attainments. Because of the past impingement and challenge of Islam and Christianity, with their Semitic, Hellenistic, and non-Indian modes, it was supposed or even taken for granted by all too many foreigners that the norms of truth and religious value traditional to their regions of development and expression would be adopted by Indian Hinduism as its own.

This is the basis for a second principle which is also obvious but often is not remembered. That is, while Western beliefs and standards in the realm of religion do have an influence, the great religions of the East possess their own standards of judgment in the matter of religion, their own standards of excellence and attainment which furnish them with criteria for measuring their own and other religions. The difficulty of fully appreciating this is readily understandable. Even if he is well versed in oriental religion, the non-Easterner by the very fact of his origin finds it difficult if not impossible to attain a high enough degree of empathy to forget the standards of his own environment.

Further, there is a prevalent tendency on the part of many, even those who know the Eastern areas of the world well, to consider the religions of these areas as peripheral factors on the present scene, elements which at the most are vestiges of the past, doomed by contemporary events to lose any influence they may now possess. Here, as we noted earlier, there is reflected both the ingrained attitude of the non-Easterner and the standards by which the Westerner has traditionally judged the vitality and relevance of a religion within its social-historical context.

This attitude manifests itself quite frequently in the judgment of both Western laity and Western scholarship that a religion such as Hinduism is not at all alive to the contemporary conditions of its particular society, and that if it possesses any life at all it expresses itself only within a philosophical-theological context or a cultic framework that is without social relevance to the peoples of its area. This judgment is not without some foundation. However, it must be counterbalanced by a third principle. This is the maxim that Hinduism does possess life to the degree that a normal characteristic of conscious life, awareness of one's surroundings, is a fact of primary importance to the religion in its present state.

These three principles—first, that Hinduism is not borrowing from the outside with the purpose of displacing that which is *essential* to its indigenous tradition; second, that the standards to which Hinduism is appealing are the very norms that are central to its own values and traditions; and, third, that Hinduism is alive to the present situation, both its dangers and its opportunities—these I believe to be essential to an understanding of the contemporary trends within Hinduism.

However, the principles must be recognized for what they are: bases for understanding and investigation, not unqualified absolutes. They possess errors common to many generalizations in that they are not true in equal or like degree for all areas of Hindu religious expression, nor are they of universal validity within all manifestations and areas of the religion. And while this must be so whenever the attempt is made to describe something so closely associated with human beings and broad social-cultural phenomena, it is especially true when one is seeking to discern trends on the part of objects which because they are alive are necessarily in a state of flux.

It is instructive at this point to note Werner Heisenberg's Principle of Indeterminacy in physics, namely, that if an electron is considered as a particle, it is apparently impossible to determine both its position and its velocity at the same time. Heisenberg concludes from this principle that, philosophically at least, there is a basic indeterminacy in reality itself, despite the fact that predictability and probability exist in the mass of things.

I will seek to describe what appear to be some important aspects of Hinduism today, aspects or trends that suggest something of the possible immediate, and perhaps the long-range, future of Hinduism. But there is an indeterminacy to it all. The fascination, the mystery—the sense of enigma that has accompanied Hindu religion and its many variations throughout the centuries remains.

CHAPTER ONE

THE NATURE
OF INDIAN
RELIGION

When one attempts to consider the nature of Indian Religion, he is immediately aware of both the enormity of the subject and his own audacity in even suggesting that he can do other than contribute further to the already prevalent generalizations and misunderstandings. The infrequent, valuable insights that result from brief and general attention to the subject are too often obscured by erroneous broad impressions instilled in the general public mind. On the other hand, detailed technical discussions of necessity are usually limited to one aspect of the subject and easily create equally false conclusions unless the discussions are limited strictly to an audience of specialists. In the one case, a list of features is presented and appears to be adequate because it is inclusive. In the other instance, a specific characteristic achieves undue prominence merely because it is chosen, and other traits are necessarily ignored.

As the student of Indian religion pursues his subject, he frequently becomes convinced that his difficulties in clearly ascertaining the nature of Indian religion are not simply those associated with similar endeavors in any study of a long-existing, many-faceted phenomenon. He may be overwhelmed by either the ambiguity of authoritative Indian voices on the matter, or by the radically varying but specific pronouncements of equally authoritative Indian scholars. As a result, some are led to conclude there is no structured "nature" belonging to Indian religion that can be captured in meaningful language. Or, convinced that there is a "nature," a describable "character" to Indian religion even though they cannot find it, others are tempted to repeat the observation of the eleventh-century Muslim scholar al-Bērūnī, recently quoted by the popular Indian iconoclast Nirad Chaudhuri, that the character of the Hindus makes it "particularly difficult to penetrate into the essential nature of any Indian subject." [1]

Succumbing only briefly to the temptation to cite at length the attempts of others to describe the primary expression of Indian religion—namely, Hinduism—at least two basic patterns are evident over the past hundred years. One, most closely associated with general Western and Christian interpretations, is typically expressed by H. D. Griswold in his *Insights into Modern Hinduism*. He lists the characteristics of Hinduism as being (1) the tendency to deify whatever is; (2) the tendency to syncretism; (3) the acceptance and justification of a pronounced contrast between priestly and popular religion; (4) the dominance of the religious point of view in all the affairs of life, or the supremacy of the religious consciousness; (5) great reverence for the ideal of renunciation and great capacity for sacrifice; and (6) the existence of aspirations and anticipations still largely unfilled and unsatisfied.[2] Griswold not only reflects the religious stance from which he writes but he also repeats much that had been established in Western minds by the time of Hegel's consideration of Hinduism in the 1830s.[3] Broad state-

[1] Nirad Chaudhuri, *The Continent of Circe* (Bombay, 1966), p. 96.
[2] H. D. Griswold, *Insights into Modern Hinduism* (New York, 1934), pp. 17 ff.
[3] G. W. F. Hegel, *Philosophy of History* (New York, 1956), p. 141.

ments are made and certain tendencies are noted. The nature and depth of Hindu religion remains unfathomed.

A second pattern of description is also well known. It is one that concentrates on the philosophical or philosophical-theological, with very little if any attention paid to the cultic and social expressions of the religion. Since we will be giving some consideration to this feature of Hinduism later we will not cite any specific examples now. The essential nature of this approach to Hindu religion (and, unfortunately, to the personal piety of the Indian people), was a concentration upon the intellectual formulations of a limited few in Indian history. The impression given has been that the sophisticated reflections of these few are the common property in one form or another of the wide mass of Indian-Hindu people, an impression that might not be totally erroneous, but that has tended to convey the idea that all Hindus are philosophically inclined and religiously sophisticated. Despite the aid this approach has given to the non-Indian seeking to understand Hinduism, the nature of Indian religion as lived by the peoples of India has not been adequately conveyed, and a misleading impression has been established.

Hindu scholars have been especially active in supporting this intellectual, philosophical interpretation of Indian religion. Recognizing the need for scholarly presentation of the philosophical-theological themes that have played an important role for over 2,500 years in Indian religious, cultural, and social life, they have frequently been led by their own association with, and understandable enthusiasm for, this aspect of Hinduism to ignore the Hinduism practiced by the mass of their coreligionists. While presenting their conception of ideal Hinduism as if it were *actual* Hinduism, in many instances they themselves have participated with sincerity in the public and private aspects of the cultic and social features of Indian religion which in their writings they have frequently ignored, as if such features were inconsequential.

These two types of interpretation of Hinduism have, of course, been partly modified by others that seek more comprehensive understanding. Even in the reporting of Abbé Dubois at the close of the eighteenth century, a beginning toward generally unbiased description of Indian social and religious life can be seen, and it has progressed to a high scholarly level in the past few decades. In some instances, even the well-meaning but somewhat prejudiced Western religious perspective has allowed itself to be informed by new currents of scholarly method and analysis. And perhaps more importantly, scholars and teachers formerly limited so largely to the philosophical in their interpretations of Hinduism have come to recognize the inadequate picture of Indian religion they have presented. Through the use of a wide variety of scholarly disciplines, and a growing awareness of the greatly different levels of Indian religious life and expression, the interpreter of Hinduism today knows that he is not confronted with merely a philosophical system surrounded by meaningless religious trappings that have accumulated over centuries. And it is to be hoped that the interpreter writing from a particular religious stance is rapidly learning the inadequacy of his former procedures and the resulting errors in his understanding.

The centrality of religious thought as expressed through classical Hindu philosophy, the importance of detailed philological analysis of the traditional texts associated with that classical expression, and the relevance of more modern attempts by Indians themselves to separate the essence of Hinduism from its many accretions—the value of none of these should be denied. However, a statement by Professor M. N. Srinivas of the University of Delhi is most pertinent at this point: "An emphasis on religious behaviour as such, as distinguished from what is written in the religious books and the opinions of the upper castes, would have provided us with a view of Hinduism substantially different from that of the philosophers, Sanskritists and reformers." [4]

Our problem, therefore, is to work toward an inclusive comprehension of the nature of Indian religion as it is found within Hin-

[4] M. N. Srinivas, *Caste in Modern India and Other Essays* (Bombay, 1962), p. 132.

duism—the collection of phenomena that today continues as the almost all-inclusive example of the Indian religious experience. While so doing we must remember that in so brief a presentation the resulting generalizations are necessarily only working hypotheses toward a more adequate understanding.

I

It is essential that a consideration of the religion of the Indian people, both of the past and of the present, take into account two strands or currents present in all religions that are long in existence, varied in expression, and large in membership. These two elements are the religious sentiments, beliefs, and acts of the people in general, *and* the core concepts that serve as a unifying foundation for the beliefs, subsequent acts, and general religious sentiments of the people identified with the particular religion. When the religion is viewed in its totality each strand is in some measure identified with the other, complementary to the other, and dependent upon the other for its own full significance in the total religious complex. Separate consideration, though necessary, is seldom wholly adequate. The interweaving of the one with the other demands that consideration of one be accompanied by an awareness of the other if the variety and complexity of Indian religion is to be comprehended.

It is not our function to repeat the many scholarly debates as to the various early sources of what is later designated "Hinduism." [5] What is apparent is that the peoples inhabiting the subcontinent before the appearance in India of the Āryans some time in the second millennium B.C. participated in practices and possessed beliefs not unlike those we know to have existed in the eastern Mediterranean and Mesopotamian areas in the same general period. And contrary to earlier scholarly opinion, it is now commonly held that

[5] For a discussion of the complex nature of the problem of "substratum theories" regarding Hinduism, see J. Gonda, *Change and Continuity in Indian Religion* (The Hague, 1965), pp. 7–37.

this type of religious thought and activity was not overwhelmed to the point of extinction in India by the appearance of the Vedic religion traditionally associated with the Āryans. Rather, much of it has continued down to the present, though frequently emerging through the centuries in new guise. It may even be that the cults of some of the major deities of today have their origins in the pre-Āryan forerunners of those deities. Whatever the case—and we are, of course, in a realm demanding careful scholarly analysis as well as informed conjecture—there is little doubt of the continued presence in India of religious beliefs and cults having origins not to be identified with the oral and written literature associated with early Āryan Vedism, Brāhmanism, or classical Hinduism.[6]

Speaking broadly, this early type of religion with its awareness of "powers" both large and small inhabiting all existence, powers intimately related to the events experienced by man, was confronted by an Āryan religion that while not totally different did, at least as we see it through the Vedas, concern itself more directly with the great powers associated with the universe of being. Generalizations at this point are hazardous, however, for the evidence as to the nature of the indigenous religion is extremely limited, while the religion of the Vedic Āryans is primarily known through a literary tradition that does not necessarily reveal all levels of Āryan religious experience. The deposits of both that are important for subsequent Indian religion are the awareness of "divine" powers in the world and the presupposition that man is in a special relationship to these powers. Certainly, up to this point there is nothing that in a specific way differentiates early Indian religion from that of other areas of the world and their cultures. Local forms or modes of expression were undoubtedly different, but the broad outline of "religious" awareness was not unique.

By the early centuries of the first millennium B.C. two major strands of development had become apparent in Indian religion. One is an emphasis upon a correct relationship with the powers by

[6] See J. H. Hutton, *Caste in India* (London, 1963), especially Appendix B, "Hinduism In Its Relation to Primitive Religions in India," pp. 223–62.

means of the cult; the recognition of certain endowed individuals as being especially fitted to guide that relationship; and an increasing concentration upon the role of human society, through these individuals, in maintaining the "proper" structure of existence. The second component is a growing tendency toward formal, structured reflection upon the nature of the human situation and its relationship to the totality of being. Here, again, early Indian religion as we know it is not absolutely different from that of other areas, though claims are occasionally made as to chronological precedence in the matter of the latter development. What is important within this context is that these two areas of emphasis have served as central axes around which much of Indian religion has revolved. The first—the cult—may broadly be considered the base around which the variety of popular mass religion clusters; the second— structured reflection—is the early manifestation of the body of intellectual expressions that has developed into the thematic foundation of Indian religion. Given the nature of traditional Asian philosophy, this latter element, usually referred to as Indian philosophy, is better understood in the West by a phrase such as "philosophy-theology." [7] It is the source of as well as the forum for the elaboration of the core concepts to which we earlier referred; while the cult serves as the vehicle for the expression of religious sentiments through worship participation.

What we are suggesting here is the beginning of a discernible distinction between what is aptly designated as the "folk religion" and the "great tradition" of a religion.[8] In the case of Indian religion, earlier foreshadowings of both are evident to the scholar; [9]

[7] Since there has been no formal distinction between philosophy and theology in traditional or contemporary Hindu thought, and because of the "religious" or "spiritual" quality of Hindu philosophy, the expression "philosophy-theology" is helpful in conveying to the Westerner the nature of what is usually termed Indian philosophy.

[8] For a helpful discussion of these two elements see Robert N. Bellah, ed., *Religion and Progress in Modern Asia* (New York, 1965), pp. xx ff.

[9] For an example of the "great tradition" see "The Hymn to Creation," *Rgveda*, X.129. S. Radhakrishnan and C. A. Moore, *A Source Book in Indian Philosophy* (Princeton, 1957), p. 23 f.

by sometime in the middle of the first millennium B.C. both had become well-established, interrelated, but yet distinct elements that have continued down to today. It was their joint but separate existence to which Professor Griswold was perhaps pointing when he cited "the acceptance and justification of a pronounced contrast between priestly and popular religion" as being a characteristic of Hinduism, though we would feel compelled to object to his selection of the term "priestly."

II

It seems wise first to consider the philosophic aspects of the great tradition of Hinduism because in this thematic cluster we have available to us more easily describable central elements that furnish clues for the understanding of Indian religion. This is not to suggest at all that the factors constituting this great tradition are uncomplex or that they lack long and varied histories of interpretation. Because we are primarily interested, as our title suggests, in modern trends, we shall have to leave to others consideration of the large and important problems about early origins and the processes of historic change and interpretation through which separate elements have gone, as well as the varying roles they have occupied in the totality of Hinduism. We cannot give attention to problems concerning their order of appearance within emerging Hinduism, nor to the details of the separate understandings of them that is, in reality, the history of the development of Indian philosophy-theology.

Early Indian reflection had sensed a pattern within existence, an order behind or within that which is experienced by man. Despite the experience of a variety of powers that frequently, if not always, seemed at odds with each other, Indian thinkers delved beneath the apparent confusion of existence to perceive a Unity. Whether understood as an impersonal Law governing the arena of being (ṛta, Dharma), or expressed in terms suggesting an ultimate deity that is more properly understood as an Absolute Principle in a philosophic sense (Brahman), this fundamental underlying "structure" has served as the core for intellectual expressions of Hinduism, the religion. This ultimate One is the source, if not the creator, of the multiplicity experienced by man, as well as the final unity that brings together variety into a cohesive whole. As such It furnishes structure and meaning, though the full nature of that meaning is beyond the understanding of limited man. In Its final essence this Ultimate defies description, though It may faintly be perceived in Its conditioned, and therefore non-Ultimate, state by conditioned man. However stated by traditional Hinduism, the Brahman conception in one fashion or another is a fundamental presupposition for the intellectual Indian-Hindu religious consciousness. It remains today at the center of philosophical-theological expressions of Hinduism, and a denial of It raises serious questions concerning the Hinduism of the denier.

A second element within the great tradition is a belief as to the nature of the ultimate essence, the "self" of man. In a fashion similar to that of the presupposition concerning Brahman, the understanding of the essential quality or element of man is an integral aspect of intellectual expressions of Hinduism. Whether it be the absolute identity of Brahman and the self (Ātman) in the Kevalādvaita associated with the thought of Śaṅkara, the identity with a distinction found in the Viśiṣṭādvaita of Rāmānuja, or the distinction within a relationship in the Dvaita system of Madhva, Hinduism continues to maintain the close ultimate relationship of the Unity (Brahman) and the self (Ātman) of man. The convictions concerning these two themes—Brahman and Ātman—have marked the predominant expressions of the intellectual Hindu tradition, and ultimately have separated from Hinduism other religious developments in India such as Jainism and Buddhism.

A further essential presupposition of the Indian religious consciousness as it has expressed itself in intellectual terms within Hinduism is concerned with the nature of empirical existence, the realm of the universe and its movement. Physical existence is understood to be a process, it is not static. The universe is involved in a succession of movements best described as cyclical, rather than linear, in that this flux or movement is one without ultimate purpose or goal. The constant change (saṁsāra) of measurable structure involves all being, and the self (Ātman) of man is entangled in the process.

Closely identified, if not identical, with the presupposition of this process, is the conception indicated by the term "karma." Every condition of being is the result of a previous cause or causes and is itself influential in determining the acts leading to further conditions or states within the process. Thus the governing principle behind the fluidity that man perceives in his environment is the same principle that ties him to that which he experiences, and in which he finds no permanent meaning or ultimate value.

What we have up to this point is the intellectual expression of the Hindu understanding of the Absolute or Ultimate, the presupposition of the essential being or essence of man, the general Indian conception of the nature of the physical, the affirmation as a certainty that men as they are now constituted in their own self-understanding are subject to an all-pervading law of cause and effect. The last two of these themes are essential in one form or another to any expression of the developed Indian religious spirit, and all four are inherent in philosophical-theological Hinduism.

However, Hindu thought does not leave man condemned to the condition these absolute presuppositions impose upon him. It must be clearly noted that Indian philosophy is basically soteriological or salvationist. Both these terms can be misleading because of their Western-Christian connotations. Nevertheless, the major expressions of Indian philosophy are concerned with the self or spirit of man and its attainment of release from its present condition.[10] And it is this aspect that gives us reason to seek some designation such as "philosophy-theology" to indicate the nature of the core of the Hindu intellectual enterprise throughout its history.

Freedom (mokṣa) from the realm of saṁsāra to which the Ātman

[10] The materialistic Cārvāka thought is the only notable exception.

is apparently, or actually, bound by the fact of karma and attainment or recognition of the proper relationship with Brahman thus constitute the *summum bonum* toward which Hindu philosophical and religious thought is always pointing. It is through these themes, in particular, that Hindu philosophy-theology becomes a source of guidance for the religious aspirations and activities of the Hindu *homo religiosus*. Having described man and the environment that limits him, its analysis of man denies the ultimate necessity of the limitation.

The foregoing can only serve as a brief indication or outline of a system of thought that is complex, varied, and subtle in its detailed content. No one can make even a small beginning toward a meaningful understanding of the nature of Indian religion without an awareness and appreciation of these intellectual convictions that have become internalized into the very being of the Hindu consciousness to the degree that they are more than intellectual or rational assumptions. These they may be, and their adherents may consider them to be intellectually defensible; but their place in Hindu religion is more that of theological-religious affirmation than of debatable philosophic postulation. It is around these themes and the various interpretations of them that the intellectual aspects of the great tradition of Indian religion revolve. It is in them that Hinduism finds the core that makes it an identifiable entity in the midst of other phenomena commonly designated as religion.

III

When we turn from the "core" presuppositions of Indian religion to a consideration of the religious sentiments, beliefs, and acts found within Hinduism we are confronted by a variety of local expressions that seem to defy description if anything less than an encyclopedia of religion is attempted. Detailed studies in one particular area or of one specific group reveal divergencies from other areas and groups similarly studied *if* emphasis is placed upon the precise expressions used and acts performed. Language differences, regional histories, and provincial customs combine to produce local religious understandings and behavior.

Adequate consideration of Indian religion requires a clear recognition of this firmly established regionalism and provincialism within India, as well as of the integrative forces that have been operative over the centuries. Without the persuasive, integrative presence of the great tradition, it is to be wondered whether Indian religion would be anything other than a multitude of local cults sharing only their dramatic awareness of "divine" or "nonhuman" powers, and demonstrating in their attempts to propitiate those powers forms of religious expression similar to those of traditionalist peoples throughout the world. The philosophical-theological themes to which we have referred have been at the center of a literary tradition associated with the higher levels of Indian society; the sentiments and acts typical of mass Hinduism have been related to those themes primarily through popular and unstructured means of diffusion that lack the sophistication of the classical literary tradition.

However, we must also recognize that forms or structures in general Hinduism that reveal a relationship to the classical core themes are not only results of a downward process from the classical tradition to the local level. As Professors Robert Redfield and Milton Singer have demonstrated, there is a continuity between a "primary" or indigenous civilization and its great tradition on the one hand, and on the other the folk culture from which it grows, wherein the more provincial or local traditions are contributors in the process of creating the overarching, more widespread culture of the unifying civilization.[11] There is a process of universalization in which local elements are brought out of their provincial limitations into a wider and more complex context of association with elements from other localities. It is certainly true, as McKim Marriott notes,

[11] Referred to in McKim Marriott, "Little Communities in an Indigenous Civilization," in McKim Marriott, ed., *Village India* (Chicago, 1969). See also "The Cultural Role of Cities," *Economic Development and Cultural Change* (October 1954), III, 53–73.

that "An indigenous great tradition remains in constant communication with its own little traditions through a sacred literature, a class of literati, a sacred geography, and the rites and ceremonies associated with each of these." [12] Yet it must be added, as he goes on to do, that the communication is a two-way process in which the local has a role in the creation of the more general, and the so-called great receives a measure of its status because it is a dependent relative of the local and not a foreign stranger. The "great tradition derives its authority from faith in its native belongingness. . . ." [13]

Generally speaking, folk Hinduism finds a primary source for its formal structure and expressions in the oral and written traditions associated with the Purāṇas and the Itihāsas, or Epics, ancient stories and chronicles that tell of creation, recite the genealogies of gods and legendary early men, and present the mythological-legendary history of ancient times. As Professor V. Raghavan states rather dramatically, "the Himalayan waters of Vedic faith and Upaniṣadic philosophy were brought to the plains of the people through several projects, the biggest of which were the Itihāsas and the Purāṇas." [14] Together these have served as a means for the communication of the great tradition in local languages through didactic myths and legends which, despite their local associations and regional varieties, knit "together into one religious society the numerous heterogeneous groups in India." [15]

Yet, even here we must be careful that we do not assume that the great and more universal Purāṇas are *the* primary foundation for local religious sentiments and behavior. Major temples have

[12] Marriott, *Village India*, p. 181.
[13] *Ibid.*, p. 196. Marriott's categories of "universalization," the upward relationship between the little traditions and the great tradition; and "parochialization," the downward relationship between the great tradition and the little traditions; and his recognition of "residual categories," content that remains indigenous and stable in either tradition are helpful in conceptualizing the intricacies of the relationships between the local and wider aspects of a "single" large culture. Cf. pp. 197 ff.
[14] V. Raghavan, "Methods of Popular Religious Instruction in South India," in Haridas Bhattacharyya, ed., *The Cultural Heritage of India* (5 vols., Calcutta, 1956), IV, 503.
[15] Srinivas, *Caste in Modern India*, p. 106.

their own local Purāṇas portraying the mythological events associated with them,[16] and these regional traditions through the course of time attain, at least locally, an identity with the larger Purāṇic deposit that is common throughout most of India. For example, in the region of the present state of Andhra the myths associated with the great temple complex at Tirupatti and the god Veṅkaṭeś-vara are influences in the formation of the religious sentiments of the people to a degree not at all equaled by the classical literary tradition, the *Bhagavadgītā,* or even the larger Purāṇas. In a more restricted locale, the myths associated with the smaller and more regional northern Andhra shrine at Siṁhachalam and its deity Narasiṁha have an influence over a more limited area of Andhra and adjacent southern Orissa. In this instance, the basic religious sentiments are received and expressed primarily through a combination of the myth tradition of the local temple at Siṁhachalam and that of the great shrine hundreds of miles away at Tirupatti.

Oscar Lewis in his study of village life notes a corresponding situation in northern India and reports his impression "that the Hindu Great Tradition is not so familiar to these villagers as one might have expected, whereas the worship of local godlings and disease goddesses, etc., is very important." [17] He joins with Marriott and others who have made similar studies in concluding that even in areas where the great tradition has been present for almost three thousand years, deities are worshipped and rituals conducted that have "no evident connection with the Great Tradition." [18] At this level, local and regional myth and legend are primary, while the pan-Hindu thematic and mythic forces appear to be of relatively little importance.

A further aspect central to folk Hinduism is illustrated by the role of rites of "initiation" or "consecration" (dīkṣā). These ceremonies are not clearly separated from the early Vedic tradition and customs derived from it, nor are they to be sharply distinguished from practices that have been closely identified with the cultic ac-

16 *Ibid.*
17 Oscar Lewis, *Village Life in Northern India* (New York, 1965), p. 236.
18 *Ibid.,* p. 235.

companiments of the great tradition. Descending from antiquity, they are of primary importance within the major Hindu groupings —Vaiṣṇava, Śaivite, and Tantric.[19] Here we have an additional element working for cohesion among the wide variety of local folk expressions. In many instances these rites are regionally observed and conceived of as being integral to all-India Hinduism, especially by the upper social levels, who are also conscious of the thematic great tradition. The unlettered Indian, whether aware of the larger associations of his actions or not, finds in these ceremonial acts a concrete embodiment of his particular status in the totality of existence and in his local community. And, while emphasis is placed upon the form of the ceremony as locally observed in order to determine the ritual purity and resulting rank of the participants within Indian Hinduism, discussion of this aspect of the dīkṣās has sometimes obscured their important role as vehicles for, and sustainers of, the individual piety and corporate religiousness of the Hindu peoples.

No discussion of folk Hinduism can safely avoid making at least a brief reference to elements frequently identified with the tribal peoples of India that on closer investigation are discovered to be integral to the parochial religion of the countryside and not limited to tribal areas alone. Understandably, the modern or educated Hindu will tend to make a sharp distinction between tribal and village conceptions of the soul, the land of the dead, the nature of the gods and spirits, the propriety of worshipping or honoring ancestors, the importance of tutelary deities, the ever-present danger of evil spirits, etc., and what he considers to be Hinduism.[20] When viewed from the perspective of the great tradition and the ceremonies associated with it, this distinction has some justification. Yet much of the folk religion of the Indian people and what they consider to be Hinduism contains these same elements in varying degrees. Just as local myth and practice are intermixed with clas-

[19] Gonda, *Change and Continuity*, pp. 315–462.
[20] E.g., Tarak Chandra Das, "Religious Beliefs of the Indian Tribes," in Bhatta-charyya, ed., *Cultural Heritage of India*, IV, 421–32.

sical Hindu thought and cult, both these latter elements are permeated by, and frequently not distinguished from, beliefs and acts the modern sophisticated Hindu conceives to be tribal and primitive.

"Pilgrimage" and "ritual purity" are two additional factors contributing to an awareness of the relationship or identity between the immediately local and the larger regional if not all-India Hinduism. Low-caste or outcaste groups in the process of rising on the social and religious scale place new emphasis on both as means of identifying themselves with the cultic aspects of the larger tradition espoused by those whose acceptance and approval they seek.[21] Ritual purity and the horror of its opposite—pollution—have been a central hallmark of traditional higher-caste Hinduism. Emulation of the religious-social standards of personal habit and behavior associated with the great tradition, and when possible use of the tradition's cultic avenues for participation in the larger community and its values, offer a means for association with that wider group and the attainment of values that can be received only from it. By sustained effort to achieve a higher level of ritual cleanliness, and by participation in activities such as pilgrimage, whereby identity with the larger community as well as fuller sharing in its values is attained, the highly parochial are brought into closer relationship with the more universal.[22]

The foregoing matters combine with an immediate awareness of divine power furnished by the Itihāsas and Purāṇas to constitute much of the Hindu religion as it has been and is lived. There are, of course, other elements that could be included if space permitted. Some, such as astrology, are central matters in much of everyday Indian life. They, or at least many of the conceptions underlying them, appear to be inherently related to an understanding of hu-

[21] See Bernard S. Cohn, "The Changing Status of a Depressed Caste," in Marriott, ed., *Village India*, pp. 74 ff.
[22] See Irawati Karve, "A Maharashtrian Pilgrimage," *Journal of Asian Studies*, XXII (November 1962), 13–29; Marriott, *Village India, passim.*; M. N. Srinivas, *Social Change in Modern India* (Berkely, 1966), *passim.*

man and cosmic existence that is an integral part of the Indian religious consciousness. Widespread belief in nonhuman powers, frequently minor or small but never inconsequential in their evil or benevolence, and ascription of one's condition to preordained fate are further instances of the close and continuing relationship between folk Hinduism and conceptions long a part of traditional man's understanding of himself and his environment. Their absence from contemporary discussions of Hindu philosophy and culture should not cause us to ignore either their role within the totality of Indian religiousness or the support for them that is present in classical Hinduism as traditionally understood.

IV

A central problem for the student of religion is the determination of the functions and relative weights of the various discernible components of his particular object of study. Closely allied is the question as to the distinctions that are perhaps present or absent among the components in the religion itself, if the latter are at all recognized as separable by adherents within the religious faith and its cult. In the case of Hinduism, for example, is the distinction between the "great tradition" and "folk religion" meaningful at all except as a system of classification for identification and analysis? Does it reflect a conscious bifurcation within the general Indian mind? Or is it rather a superimposition by a minority elite within the religion and by external observers? Our use of these categories, which I believe to be defensible as an aid to understanding, should not be allowed to obscure an essential unity wherein, as we have suggested, the two categories are in constant interrelationship. This relationship is one of mutual dependence as well as productive tension; it is one in which subtle and covert values transfer from one to the other. The end product, when viewed from the not always self-conscious perspective of the majority of adherents, is an integrated body of beliefs and actions that serve not as *possible* keys to a proper understanding of the human situation, but rather *the* correct beliefs and *the* appropriate conduct made absolutely imperative because these beliefs are internalized as life-sustaining verities—verities having their source in dimensions not at all limited to the conditioned arena of man's immediate environment.

CHAPTER TWO

THE
RECENT
PAST

A leading Indian has written that "the most casual observer can see that without the reformation of Hinduism on a broad basis Indian independence would not have been possible." [1] Whether this assertion is justified may be debated by some; nevertheless, there can be no question that the immediate past history, the present condition, and perhaps the unknown future prospects of Indian society, culture, and political activity have a close relational dependence upon Hinduism. An awareness of this and of the equally obvious fact that Hinduism as the predominate religion of India is inextricably involved with the present of the subcontinent and new nation of India are essential for an adequate perception of the recent Hindu-Indian past.

I

Numerous accounts have been written of the nineteenth-century religious, cultural, and social ferment within the subcontinent of

[1] K. M. Panikkar, *The Foundations of New India* (London, 1963), p. 46.

India. Whether written from the perspective of the apologist, the critic, or the assumed independent observer, they all testify to a process of movement and change wherein Hindu religion and Indian society were made to confront a variety of forces identified primarily with the West. It was during this period that what has been termed "Westernization" became most clearly apparent. The process has continued and today manifests itself throughout much of Indian society, particularly at the higher social and economic levels, though now it is more adequately described by the term "modernization."

At the beginning of the nineteenth century, India as a geographical area was rapidly coming under the military-political control of Great Britain. This and the equally well-recognized encroachment of European civilization into the area have sometimes served to obscure the religious-cultural-social condition at the time of the early British military successes. Generally speaking, it was a situation in which what might properly be termed "Hindu" religion was existent but dormant, expressing itself in age-old ways with little cognizance of the resources at its roots or the foreign influences that were beginning to gather around it.

At the level of what we have termed the "great tradition"—that is, the perennial philosophical-theological themes associated with Sanskrit literature—the heritage was the property of the intellectual few, as well as the partial possession of the upper "varṇa," or societal groups, whose religious orthodoxy rested largely upon that tradition and its cultic accompaniment. However, that inheritance served primarily as a conservative but cohesive means of preservation for that which was established by tradition, both intellectually and socially. There is little if any indication of a conscious awareness at the end of the eighteenth century that the times were markedly different from any in the past. For the intellectual, the categories of thought were the same as those of many centuries before, and they were expressed in the mode or guise associated with the classical philosophers. There had been little change in five hundred or a thousand years, and in large measure the foundations upon which Indian thought rested were little different from what they had been in the Upaniṣadic age over two thousand years before.

The Kevalādvaita thought associated with the great sage Śaṅkara (circa 800), the Viśiṣṭādvaita of Rāmānuja (circa 1100), and the Dvaita of Madhva (circa 1250) existed as philosophies, and along with other traditional systems of thought were a part of what are now designated the "Six Schools" of Indian philosophy. In some instances these three systems had served as the philosophical-theological base for popular religious movements or awakenings, with the result that these three expressions of the tradition and its themes served, and have continued to serve, as the wellsprings upon which intellectual Hindu religion drew.

Coupled with this intellectual heritage, particularly in the north of India, there was the not easily measured Muslim contribution to the whole of Indian culture. A few writers have tended to portray this contribution in an idealized form and in some instances gloss over deep-rooted tensions while glorifying the Islamic contribution.[2] Nevertheless, the presence of Islam as an integrated religion and culture, with its ideal if not always actualized religious-social identity, must not be ignored. Though the antipathies between the great traditions of the two religious cultures were great and the folk atmospheres created tensions that cannot be minimized, both expressed themselves in a common area possessing a homogeneity that demanded accommodation and actual if not always admitted compromise. The fact of Sikhism and a careful analysis of its various roots attests to this. As Humayun Kabir states it, perhaps too extremely, "It is indeed difficult to say how much of the present world outlook of the Hindu is derived from the Vedas and Upanishads and how much from the teachings of Islam."[3] True, the Islamic political and social structure in large measure lived removed from the Hindu society over which it reigned, but the the-

[2] E.g., Bipin Chandra Pal, *Keshab Chandra Sen and the Making of Modern India* (Calcutta, 1893).
[3] Humayun Kabir, *The Indian Heritage* (Bombay, 1955), p. 66.

ology and cult that was at its base did not remain absolutely confined to the same structures. As a result, the Hindu religious ferment of the nineteenth century was in part indebted to the religion of its non-Hindu overlords.

A further and primary element of Hindu religious thought at the beginning of the nineteenth century was a heritage of accommodation between the thematic philosophical-theological tradition and the folk religion. It is necessary to be cautious here, for overstatement can convey the wrong impression. Yet Indian religious history and development will be misunderstood, and Hinduism's capability for change unfathomed, if this is not carefully noted. In our discussion of the nature of Indian religion we have touched on the intricacies involved in the simultaneous separation and interaction of the two. What we are now calling attention to is a long history wherein popular religious movements had risen out of expressions, not always sophisticated, of various understandings of the classical thought of Hinduism. The "bhakti" movements spreading over central and northern India with their dependence, frequently hardly known by their adherents, upon classical philosophical-theological formulations; and the popular Śaivism, especially of the South, for which a similar indebtedness was true—these groups and their newly developed traditions constituted a working base for the development that was to occur in the nineteenth and twentieth centuries. Popular mass religion was at least in a limited degree receptive to larger horizons, and in the wider view possessed some measure of adaptability to regionalized and localized interpretation.

II

The first dramatic indication of the beginning of a possible new course for Hinduism was the founding of the Brāhmo Samāj (Society of God) in 1828. Much has been written about the Samāj and its founder, Ram Mohan Roy.[4] The story of its inception,

[4] A partial listing, for example: W. M. Bell, *Rammohan Roy* (Calcutta, 1933); Ramananda Chatterjee, *Ram Mohan Roy and Modern India* (Calcutta, 1918); Sophia D. Collett, *Life and Letters of Raja Ram Mohan Roy* (Calcutta, 1913);

ideals, and subsequent stormy history is in large measure an account of the development of what has been properly termed the liberalizing current in nineteenth-century and subsequent Hinduism.

The experience of Ram Mohan Roy's sixty-one years of life (1772–1833) is a microcosmic reproduction of the forces that were to be active in the liberalizing wing of Hinduism from his time onward. Born a Brāhman and raised as an orthodox Hindu, Ram Mohan prepared for the civil service. The necessities of this preparation and his own scholarly bent quickly brought him into close contact with Islamic and British culture. An early mastery of the languages associated with these traditions and a firm grounding in his own Hindu heritage endowed him with the ability to see his own contemporary religious-cultural environment both from the outside perspective and from that of the environment's own rich past.

The end result was an individual prepared to lead like-minded Indians in a reform of Hinduism. Some have placed a large amount of emphasis upon the Christian aspects of Ram Mohan's thought and the ideas of the Brāhmo Samāj, and others point to the Muslim ethos in his religious-cultural background. But undue stress upon these can easily lead to a misunderstanding of the Samāj and of liberal Hinduism in subsequent decades. Rather, his thought and the Brāhmo expression of it was, in the words of an Indian writer, a "synthesis of the doctrines of the European Enlightenment with the philosophical views of the Upanishads." [5] Operating from a base largely dependent upon the intellectual aspects of the great tradition of Hinduism, Ram Mohan and his colleagues entered both the intellectual and the social conflicts of their time and expressed the tradition in a manner and by a program that was European in much of its orientation.

J. N. Farquhar, *Modern Religious Movements in India* (New York, 1913); Nicol Macnicol, *Raja Ram Mohan Roy* (Madras, 1919); F. Max Müller, *Ram Mohan to Ramakrishna* (Calcutta, 1952); Romain Rolland, *Prophets of New India* (London, 1930); S. Sastri, *History of the Brahmo Samaj* (Calcutta, 1909).
[5] Panikkar, *Foundations of New India,* p. 27.

In the years immediately prior to the creation of the Brāhmo Samāj, Ram Mohan was active in religious and philosophical discussions, particularly in the Bengal area. Through speaking and writing he sought the removal of such entrenched customs as satī and rampant polytheistic ritualism, which he considered not only to be evils in themselves but also to lack any base in Vedāntic monotheism. He demonstrated his more than superficial knowledge of Christianity, and incidentally his affection for it, in frequent controversies with Christian missionaries.

All this activity reached its zenith within the framework of the early Brāhmo Samāj. Reflecting the various influences mentioned above that were at work within early nineteenth-century India, the primary manifesto of the Samāj, written by Ram Mohan, reveals something of the aims and spirit of himself and his colleagues.

No graven image shall be brought in the Samāj. No sermon, discourse, prayer or hymn shall be delivered except such as may have a tendency to promote the contemplation of the Author and Preserver of the Universe, to the furtherance of charity, morality, piety, benevolence, virtue and the strengthening of the bonds of union between men of all religious persuasions and creeds. No object, animate or inanimate, that has been or is . . . an object of worship shall be reviled, or spoken of slightingly and contemptuously.[6]

The monotheistic emphasis in Ram Mohan's thought was a dual product of his early studies of Islam and his conviction that such a monotheism was at the heart of Upaniṣadic-Vedāntic teaching. While there is no question that Christian theism had its influence, many Christian writers have emphasized this to the neglect of the Hindu and Muslim sources for it. The Christian position and challenge may have hastened the birth of the expression of the thought, but the thought itself was in large measure native to the Indian soil of the time, both Hindu and Muslim.

Inherent in this monotheistic emphasis and its relatively uncomplex structure was the belief that true religion rests upon two basic supports. These foundations—faith in a single creative Di-

[6] Trust Deed of Brāhmo Samāj of 1830.

vine of infinitely benevolent Nature, and belief in the immortal nature of the souls of men—are all that are needed for the emergence of pure religion. Human faith in that Divine frees the individual from the confines of degrading ritualism and sanctified custom, and leaves him free to honor the Divine through service to his fellow man.

This position, combined with the desire to purge Hinduism at its cultic and social-custom levels from practices that were considered degrading and without foundation in the great tradition, created a base which remains today as the platform for "liberal" Hinduism. While the Brāhmo Samāj itself ceased to be a viable organizational force even in the nineteenth century, its theoretical monotheism and its cry for cultic reform still remain as a creative legacy.

There is, however, a further aspect of the thought of Ram Mohan Roy which is of primary significance in contemporary Hinduism, particularly since Hinduism is now expressing itself beyond its traditional geographic borders. Much of the emphasis upon the sameness or common core of all great religions that we are accustomed to hearing from Hindu spokesmen to the West was first expressed in modern times by Ram Mohan. In a pamphlet entitled *Universal Religion,* published in 1829, and in earlier writings, he repeatedly called attention to the widespread conception of one Supreme and Eternal Being. It was his contention that the universality of this belief should be used to break down the barriers separating men, their religions, and their societies; at the same time, however, he was wise enough to recognize the need for localized expressions of the universal perception of the One. His firm conviction that God is One no matter how addressed, conceived, or worshipped was a nineteenth-century statement of the ancient Vedic cry, "That which is, is One; sages speak of It in manifold ways" [7] —a concept now expressed in the spirit of the European Enlightenment. And while this concept is not found in a meaningful way at the level of folk religion (though the theory may be operative there

[7] *Ṛgveda,* I.164.46.

also) Ram Mohan's fervent commitment to it has remained at the center of modern liberal Hinduism.

The history of the Brāhmo Samāj was in many ways a stormy one. Leadership of the group and similar or offshoot ones ranged from the saintly Bengali, Debendranath Tagore (1817–1905), who was led somewhat hesitatingly to deny that Vedic infallibility was supported by ancient tradition,[8] to the admirable Mahārāṣṭrian Judge Mahadev Govind Ranade (1842–1901) with his reasoned theism,[9] and reached its climax in the enigmatic figure of Keshab Chandra Sen (1838–1884).[10] The latter, a religious genius whose stormy career was marked by an erratic brilliance but little enduring coherence of thought or program, was particularly adept at synthesizing the varying strains of Hindu-Muslim-Christian religion present in mid-nineteenth-century India.

The Brāhmo Samāj and similar less well known groups have been characterized as the "reform" movements of early modern Hinduism in contradistinction to other organizations and currents of thought labeled "revivalist." Such distinctions, while perhaps helpful in a broad sense, can confuse the issue if they are taken as absolute without qualification. Certainly, some of the movements placed great emphasis upon reform of both the current understanding of the great tradition and the cultic-social aspects of mass Hinduism. In so doing they are understood correctly to be reformist in nature, but their sometime use or adaptation of non-Hindu norms and concepts tends to conceal from view the indigenous Indian roots to which they also turned for support. Their zeal to reform did not arise only from their recognition that such was

[8] D. Tagore, *The Autobiography of Debendranath Tagore* (Calcutta, 1909).

[9] For Ranade and the Prārthana Samāj see, e.g., J. N. Farquhar, *Modern Religious Movements in India* (New York, 1915), pp. 74 ff.; M. G. Ranade, "Importance of Social Reforms," in K. P. Karunakaran, *Religion and Political Awakening in India* (Meerut, 1965), Appendix L.; and D. S. Sarma, *Hinduism Through the Ages* (Bombay, 1961), chapter XI (A revised and abridged edition of Sarma's *Renaissance of Hinduism*).

[10] For K. C. Sen see, among others, Farquhar, *Modern Religious Movements;* F. Max Müller, *Ram Mohan to Ramakrishna;* P. C. Mozumdar, *Life and Teachings of Keshub Chandra Sen* (Calcutta, 1887); Pal, *Keshab Chandra Sen;* Sarma, *Hinduism;* T. E. Stater, *Khesab Chandra Sen and the Brahmo Samaj* (Madras, 1884).

needed. We miss their significance if we overlook their firm conviction that there was something of infinite value to be revived through the act of purification.

So, too, with those individuals and movements labeled revivalist. They sought to revive what they held to be the correct understanding of Hinduism, and in so doing they were usually defensive and at the same time critical of non-Indian sources of thought and modes of activity. However, their defensive and largely antiforeign posture did not prevent a remarkable degree of reforming zeal within the area of Hindu thought and cult. In fact, the concern for revival demanded that distinctions be made as to what should be revived.

Perhaps the primary difference between the revivalists and the reformers was in the sources of authority to which they looked for their standards of thought and action.[11] The latter placed much emphasis upon the guidance of human reason as a companion authority to the Indian-Hindu heritage; as has been suggested, the European Enlightenment, with its emphasis upon reason, served for them as the standard for determining the values and disvalues of that heritage. The revivalists, on the other hand, found the authority for their doctrines and work in the Indian-Hindu heritage itself, with the standard for the judgment of that broad, amorphous heritage to be found in what was firmly held to be the divinely revealed core of the heritage. This last point is of great importance and must not be overlooked. The non-Hindu must never forget the central role of divine revelation within Hinduism in general and in dynamic expressions of Hindu vitality in particular.

The leading instance of revivalism is that of the Ārya Samāj (Society of the Āryans) and its founder Dayānand Saraswatī (1824–1883).[12] On the basis of his studies in what he held to be

---

[11] Lajpat Rai, *Lala Lajpat Rai: The Man and His Word* (Madras, 1907), pp. 118 f.

[12] Among the many writings on Dayānand and the Ārya Samāj the following are helpful: Diwan Chand, *The Arya Samaj: What it is and what it stands for* (1942); Farquhar, *Modern Religious Movements*, pp. 101 ff.; Lajpat Rai, *A History of the Arya Samaj* (London, 1915); Dayanand Saraswati, *Autobiography*, ed. by

the only source of true religion, the Vedas, Dayānand was convinced that most of what constituted the Hinduism of his time was added after the great Vedic period of Indian religion. Not only did the additions lack a Vedic base, but they also perverted the truth and value inherent in the Vedas. Therefore, at the same time that it was necessary to revive the Vedic teaching itself, it was absolutely necessary as a corollary to purge contemporary Hinduism of evil accretions in thought and practice. As a result, Dayānand was as passionate in his criticism of much that was accepted as Hinduism by his fellow religionists as he was of non-Indian religion and culture.

While most, if not all, terms for labeling the thought and programs of individuals and groups must be general and are therefore easily misleading, the designation "liberal" which we used in reference to Ram Mohan does indicate the breadth of openness and adaptability that characterized the Brāhmo Samāj and its leading members during the movement's days of greatest strength. In the instance of Dayānand and the Ārya Samāj the designation "conservative," in contradistinction to the liberalism represented by the Brāhmo Samāj, is perhaps even more appropriate as a description. Founded in 1875, the Ārya Samāj was, and has continued to be, the vehicle for the expression of Dayānand's passionate cry for the revival of the Hinduism of the Vedas in religion and in wider areas of Indian life. Ignoring the later literature that was the more immediate source of the great tradition—the Upaniṣads with the commentary writings of the classical Hindu thinkers and the *Bhagavadgītā* that many of Dayānand's spiritual descendents today find of such immense value—Dayānand held that only in the Vedas themselves was truth to be found. They alone are the direct revelation from God and, as such, offer direct insight into truth. The watchword "Back to the Vedas" is thus based upon the assurance that in them is the eternal truth that is applicable to all ages.

H. P. Blavatsky (Madras, 1952); Har Bilas Sarda, *Life of Dyananda Saraswati* (Ajmer, 1946); B. B. Sarda, ed., *Dayanand Commemoration Volume* (Ajmer, 1933); Sarma, *Hinduism*.

In attempting to analyze the fifty-one articles of faith which Dayānand used to summarize his teachings in his *Satyārtha Prakāśa* (Elucidation of True Principles), D. S. Sarma notes first and foremost this Vedic base and then those aspects of his teachings that, according to Dayānand, flow from this authority.[13] Briefly stated, there is one great God, Brahman, the Paramātman, the Supreme Spirit; there is also the immortal soul that is distinct from God and yet related to God "as the pervader and the pervaded"; and finally, there is the material cause of the universe, "prakṛti" or matter. Because of ignorance the soul is bound to the world, which is created out of prakṛti by the creative energy of God, and the soul is doomed to suffering until freed from prakṛti as a result of the practice of Dharma (justice and truth), the proper worship of God as revealed in the Vedas, and the following of the "saṁskāras" or rites that foster the physical, mental, and spiritual enrichment of man. Both the Ārya emphasis upon the saṁskāras and its use of the "śuddhi" or purification rite whereby non-Hindus are taken into Hinduism served to give the Samāj a conservative but dynamic character, the former because it reinforced traditional rites that were in one form or another spread throughout various levels of Hinduism, and the latter in that it represented an aggressive attempt to bring back into Hinduism peoples lost primarily to Indian Islam.

There has been considerable discussion about the role played by the thought of Dayānand and the activities of the Ārya Samāj in the creation of a preparatory spirit for the later Indian independence movement. Professor Sarma, for example, emphasizes the concept of "saṅghatan" or union, saying that "it implies in the programme of the Arya Samaj the organization of Hindus for self-defence. . . . This militant spirit of the Samaj has introduced into Hindu society a tone of manliness and a sense of self-respect which it lost during the centuries of Muslim rule." [14] Professor K. P. Karunakaran of the Indian School of International Studies, while referring to various charges and countercharges and governmental

---

[13] *Ibid.*, p. 86 ff.   [14] *Ibid.*, p. 92.

investigations of the Ārya Samāj during British rule, comes to the conclusion that "the charge that the Arya Samaj as an organisation, was committed to political movements of an anti-government nature was baseless, but the total effect of its propaganda in relation to the raising of national pride was conducive to the strengthening of a political movement aimed at the liberation of the Indian people from a foreign government." [15]

We shall be considering the role of Hinduism within the contemporary political context in a later chapter. However, no discussion of the formative currents of the last one hundred or more years is adequate without reference to the important part played by the more specifically religious movements in creating an atmosphere conducive to the development of an Indian political consciousness. We are aware today of the close interrelationship between religion, culture, and community, particularly as it manifests itself within nonurban, nonindustrial societies. When there is ferment in one part of the total organism there is related action or reaction throughout the whole. The movements of religious reform and revival in both liberal and conservative forms played an important part in bringing about a new pride in things Indian and a determination to express the Indian heritage freely in the political and social realms as well as in that of religion. It is no exaggeration to say that many, if not all, of the important religious movements within Hinduism in the last century had a direct or an indirect part in the creation of the political consciousness that was to become so prominent in the twentieth century.

One outstanding instance of a religious group that contributed to the growing political consciousness was the Theosophical Society founded, interestingly enough, in New York City in 1875 by non-Indians. Under the guidance of its founders, Madame Helena Blavatsky and Colonel H. S. Olcott, it later transferred its activities to India. Its concern with the religious occult was claimed to be founded upon the revelations given to Madame Blavatsky by mysterious great Masters hidden from ordinary mortals in the recesses of the Himālayas and Tibet.

[15] Karunakaran, *Religion and Political Awakening,* p. 87.

Greatly enamored of things Indian and Eastern, Theosophy expressed its teachings publicly in the language of Indian religion and philosophy (both Hindu and Buddhist), contending that Indian philosophic speculation and Hindu spirituality were the most rewarding means of achieving universal human insight into ultimate truth. While theoretically Theosophy did not limit itself to Indian thought and teaching, holding that "Theosophy is the body of truths which form the basis of all religions, and which cannot be claimed as the exclusive possession of any," [16] in actuality its European leadership identified itself more and more with India.

The fanciful aberrations of traditional Hindu thought that came to be typical of Theosophy did not, however, prevent the Society from playing an important role in the growing religious, cultural, and political self-consicousness of the Indian people. Under the subsequent leadership of an Englishwoman, Mrs. Annie Besant, Theosophy not only praised the cultural heritage of India but also sought by concrete religious and educational activity to make that heritage more visible and vital to the Indians themselves. In so doing it gave the educated Indian a sense of pride in India's culture and religion he had seldom, if ever, felt before. Even foreigners were now saying that Hindu philosophy-theology was of supreme value to all mankind! Should not the people who had been the possessors of this treasure for millennia be free politically? Were they not endowed with an awareness of divine truth that gave them a stature even superior to other peoples? And did they not have in their own history a record of self-government and social-cultural attainment that clearly established their ability to govern themselves well without the interference of foreign powers?

Aided by the rapidly developing European-Indian scholarly awareness of India's past, Theosophy and religious groups more specifically Hindu were at the forefront in calling attention to the values, and often the superiority, of things Indian. The extremity of these claims in some instances can only be excused in the light of the previous sense of inadequacy and frustration in the face of

[16] Annie Besant, "Theosophical Society," in James Hastings, ed., *Encyclopedia of Religion and Ethics* (13 vols, New York, 1951), XII, 304.

Western political and cultural domination that had so deeply permeated the Indian-Hindu consciousness.

The educated Indian had found a cultural and religious base
from which he could proceed with pride as he began with renewed
strength to make his claim for full political stature as a free person.
It was in his culture and his religion, his Indian Hinduness that his
worth and that of the Indian "nation" (an almost new concept for
the peoples of the subcontinent) was to be found.

There are two men of the nineteenth century who together combine much of what we have been discussing, Rāmakrishna and
Vivekānanda.[17] Both of them, as well as the Rāmakrishna Vedānta
Mission that resulted from their thought and activity, have been
the subject of many studies.

Rāmakrishna Paramahaṁsa (1836–1886) is the epitome of the
God-intoxicated human being who through his genius both revives
a traditional religious faith and channels it into new or more viable
directions. Briefly stated, as a result of his religious experiences,
Rāmakrishna, an unlettered mystic, came to the conclusion that
the Ultimate Divine may be approached by any form or tradition
of worship if that tradition is followed with sincere devotion. On
the basis of his own attempts to immerse himself into the Muslim
and Christian traditions which resulted, he held, in visions of Muhammad and Jesus, he proclaimed all religions to be relatively
true.

Struggling within the framework of traditional Hinduism, he
achieved his own mystical experience and the freedom from worldly
attachment which is the mark of the sannyāsī. Not only were other
religions viable paths to spiritual realization, but within Hinduism
itself, to quote a Rāmakrishna swāmī, the "various paths—jñāna,
karma, bhakti and yoga,—all lead to the same goal, if followed

[17] The list of writings about Rāmakrishna and Vivekānanda by swāmīs of the
Rāmakrishna Mission and others is almost endless. The following it only a brief
sampling: Bhupendranath Datta, *Swami Vivekananda, Patriot-Prophet* (Calcutta,
1954); Farquhar, *Modern Religious Movements;* "M" (Mahendranath Gupta),
The Gospel of Sri Ramakrishna (Madras, 1947); F. Max Müller, *Ram Mohan to
Ramakrishna;* Max Müller, ed., *Ramakrishna, His Life and Sayings* (New York,
1899); Romain Rolland, *The Life of Ramakrishna* (Calcutta, 1954); Vivekananda,
The Complete Works of Swami Vivekananda (8 vols., Calcutta, n.d.).

with steady zeal and application, and no colour, caste, creed or sex is any the least bar to the sacred temple of realization." [18] This emphasis upon universalism within Hinduism itself and the rejection of personal barriers to spiritual or religious attainment were the two primary factors that were to give the teachings of Rāmakrishna and the work of his followers the dynamism and broad appeal they still possess today in India.

Among the young men attracted to Rāmakrishna, one in particular, Narendranāth Datta (1863–1902), was to serve as the organizer, spokesman, formulator, and disseminator of the unstructured but electrifying message of his master. Obviously a brilliant and dynamic person, the young man, as Swāmī Vivekānanda, became the spokesman for modern Hinduism both in India and the West. His organizational leadership resulted in the firm establishment of the Rāmakrishna Vedānta Society and Mission, with varied religious and social activities in India and facilities for the preaching of its message around the world.

As is true in discussing many of the outstanding figures of nineteenth- and twentieth-century Hinduism, one is tempted to embark upon a detailed consideration of Vivekānanda to reveal his teachings and to consider his contribution as a reviver of Hinduism as a viable way of life and an appealing locus of allegiance to contemporary Indians. Since we must be brief and selective, it is the latter—that is, the prophet of a new Hinduism, and therefore the prophet of a new India—that particularly deserves our attention.

In a penetrating essay entitled "Vivekananda and Indian Nationalism," [19] Professor Ainslie Embree points to the following productive elements in Vivekānanda's teaching. First, Vivekānanda recognized that modern scientific culture, while associated with the West, was not in itself an attack upon the traditional Hindu religious-cultural values but was, rather, a neutral element; "it

[18] Swami Tejasananda, "Swami Vivekananda and His Message," in R. C. Majumdar, ed., *Swami Vivekananda Centenary Memorial Volume* (Calcutta, 1963), p. 45.
[19] Ainslie Embree, "Vivekananda and Indian Nationalism," in Majumdar, ed., *Vivekananda Centenary*, pp. 519–24.

could enrich, not weaken Indian life." Further, Vivekānanda more than any of the many religious and political leaders of his time and before, more "clearly, and for his time, more usefully" asserted India's greatness. He "accepted the Hindu tradition in all its complexity and richness," thereby removing the feeling of shame and humility that marked the thinking Indian of the time. And, finally, he restored to the Hindu a sense of pride in the Hindu past.

When we examine the foregoing factors together, we note that each contributed to the last one, and this new-found sense of pride has particularly marked Hinduism since Vivekānanda's day. It is for this reason that such a large number of Hindu college and university students today cite Swāmī Vivekānanda as the Hindu thinker and leader they most admire.[20] Something of the defensive spirit that had characterized Hindu leadership was removed by the Swāmī's assertion that Indian life was as adaptable as Western society to scientific discovery and implementation. Because the variety of Hindu religious cult and thought was accepted, even those matters which had been under severe attack by both reform and revivalist leaders no longer caused either shame or emotion-filled protests in their defense. India possessed a religion, a culture, and a social base giving her equal, and perhaps superior, status among the world's communities.

We must remark at this point that while the movement arising from the religious experience of Rāmakrishna and the intellectual and organizational brilliance of Vivekānanda may not be as significant as its more devout adherents claim, there can be no question about its central role in the development of contemporary Hinduism. As the reviver of intellectual expressions of Hindu religious thought among the educated, as a schoolmaster of Hindu tradition in modern guise, and as the exponent and practitioner of charitable attitudes and deeds in Indian society, the Rāmakrishna Vedānta movement more than any other one religious movement in this century has taken the lead in bringing Hindu religion into the twentieth century and its far-reaching modernizing currents.

A more contemporary Hindu thinker, Śrī Aurobindo (1872–

[20] See *infra* p. 68.

1950) developed a mystic philosophy that attracted the intellectual Indian of the middle decades of the twentieth century. Like other religious thinkers and organizers we have mentioned, he added strength to the renewed vitality of modern Hinduism. A unique and yet not totally atypical mixture of East and West, Aurobindo spent fourteen years in England obtaining an education. After graduating from Cambridge with honors, he returned to India and began his adult life as a civil servant and as an educator under the patronage of the ruler of a native state. Political events soon caught his undivided attention, with the result that he became a fiery leader in the nationalistic movement and its activities in Bengal. However, a variety of events and his own mystical, philosophical, and literary interests led him in 1910 to retire from British India to the French area of Pondicherry on the Bay of Bengal, where he followed a life of meditation and writing until his death.

Aurobindo's early training in the classical tradition of the West and his later deep study of Hindu thought were brought together in a brilliant and attractive literary style to describe the "integral yoga" or philosophy that was at the heart of his meditative reflections. The educated Westernized (modernized?) Hindu has been greatly attracted by the fusion of the classical cultures of both East and West in Aurobindo's thought and by its mode of expression, as well as by the synthetic nature of the thought itself. Briefly stated, Aurobindo's thought was based upon the conviction that ultimate truth can only be attained from the intuitive mystic vision that results from the meditative life, although he did give reason and the sciences that result from it a place in human life. When one is prepared to follow the path of meditation, then, and only then, is illumination received.

The truth gained from this illumination, as expressed by Aurobindo, is one of significant appeal to the modernized Hindu intellectual concerned with the reality of thoughts and events in the world. Denying vigorously the "illusionist" understanding of the empirical world attributed to the Vedānta of Śaṅkara, he held that the material at even its least structured levels is not without the presence of the Absolute Spirit. The degree of that presence varies, but throughout all finitude the Absolute is present with the dynamic potentiality of lifting the veil that hides It from observation within the finite. It is man's basic mission and his challenge to realize by intensive meditation the highest potential of his fundamental nature—the *divine life* that results from the attainment of a "supermind." This supermind is beyond the threshold of the ordinary mind. But it is there as a possibility because of the presence of the Absolute Spirit in all things. When the divine life is realized among men then the Spirit will truly reign in the finite world. The material has meaning and ultimate significance because of the presence of the Absolute. When that presence is known in the highest degree possible for man through the reception and development of his supermind then all things are possible. This is true Vedānta, and this is the message of Hinduism to all mankind.

Here is a recognition of the importance of the empirical world and human activity within it that to the minds of a growing number of Hindu intellectuals is commensurate with their needs as they participate as members of an active society in the modern world. Despite the fact that the message and philosophy of Śrī Aurobindo are limited in their impact to a segment within the Hindu upper classes, they are making a significant contribution to the philosophy-theology of contemporary Hinduism.[21]

A much more widely known Hindu during the first half of the present century was, of course, Mahātma Gāndhī (1869–1948). In the West, in particular, he immediately comes to mind when one considers modern India, its recent history, and the present trends which may very likely shape its future. He is remembered by middle-aged and older people in the West as one of the truly remarkable men of this or any century, and Western youth in some areas have learned of his thought and techniques for bringing about social change through attempts to adapt it to social struggles in the West. Of his central role in India's struggle for political independence

[21] Aurobindo's own writings and those of his followers are voluminous. See, for example, his *Essays on the Gītā, The Ideal of Human Unity, The Life Divine, Savitri—a Legend and a Symbol, The Synthesis of Yoga,* etc. These are published in Calcutta by the Arya Publishing House or in Pondicherry by the Sri Aurobindo Ashram.

there can be no doubt. Equally certain, and in the minds of many more important, is his place as the primary apostle of "nonviolence," "noncooperation," or "satyāgraha," which he defined by saying that "Truth (Satya) implies Love, and Firmness (Agraha) engenders and therefore serves as a synonym for force . . . that is to say, the Force which is born of Truth and Love or Non-violence." [22]

However, when one is endeavoring to ascertain the Mahātma's place within the development and shaping of the contemporary religion of India, it is not at all clear how he should be judged. True, he was intensely religious and sought to infuse the political policies and actions of himself and his colleagues with religious principles. Characteristically equating truth with religion, he said that "my devotion to Truth has drawn me into the field of politics and I can say without the slightest hesitation and yet in all humility, that those who say that religion has nothing to do with politics do not know what religion means." [23]

Western writers who have greatly admired Gāndhī as a religious person and political leader have all too often assumed that his influence upon Hindu religion was, and is, far greater than careful investigation establishes as being the case. One rather widely read book on Hinduism by a Western scholar makes a number of extreme but not atypical assertions concerning the impact Gāndhī had upon Hinduism.

It was plain that the deathknell of the old orthodoxy had already sounded and that the new "orthodoxy" as preached and lived by the Mahātma was about to take its place. . . . he was yet the greatest reformer Hinduism had ever seen. . . . he absorbed the ethical teaching of the Sermon on the Mount and the transcendent monotheism of Islam into his own Hindu life and through himself he transmitted it to the whole of India. . . . after Gandhi Hinduism will never be the same again.[24]

It is certainly not our intent to attempt to detract from the high opinion of Mahātma Gāndhī held by so many in both the East and

[22] M. K. Gandhi, *Satyagraha in South Africa* (Madras, 1928), pp. 172–73.
[23] M. K. Gandhi, *The Story of My Experiments With Truth* (London, 1949), pp. xi–xii.
[24] R. C. Zaehner, *Hinduism* (New York, 1966), pp. 174–85, *passim*.

the West. From almost any perspective, he is worthy of the great admiration bestowed upon him. However, the attempt to ascertain his impact upon Hindu religion must not be clouded by the admiration he deserves are a religious person and as a man possessing qualities of great political leadership.

The overwhelming evidence in the third decade after his death is that Gāndhī did not bestow upon Hinduism a new orthodoxy, nor did he succeed in transmitting his religious beliefs and practices to the whole of India (in fact, there is serious question that he sought to do so). And now, after his fascinating and admirable life, there is little to indicate that Hinduism is perceptibly different because of that life.

Even in the political sphere, where his leadership and impact were much more obvious during his lifetime, the legacy of his influence continues to diminish rapidly as the Gāndhīan generation forgets its heritage and also disappears from the Indian scene. For the young, with some notable exceptions, the figure of the Mahātma has assumed a status not unlike, by analogy, the traditional American view of George Washington and Abraham Lincoln. The title of an article written by the New York Times' correspondent in New Delhi on the occasion of Gāndhī's centenary in 1969 is without question a most apt statement of his place in the greater part of Indian life. It reads, "India Finds Gandhi Inspiring and Irrelevant." [25] True, vocal homage is given to him by many of the traditional leaders of some Indian political parties; and occasionally appeals are made for the support of a particular party or program claimed to be in the Gāndhīan tradition. However, a realistic view of the situation supports the journalist's statement that "lost in the vastness of India and forgotten by her, are small bands of Gandhians trying to practice what he preached." [26]

Two scholars stated succinctly and with much accuracy the political-religious impact of Gāndhī's work, and incidentally that of others we have been discussing, when they wrote:

[25] Joseph Lelyveld, New York Times Magazine, May 25, 1969, pp. 27 ff.
[26] Ibid., p. 58.

The conception of India as a spiritual nation formulated in the nineteenth and twentieth century by Dayanand, Vivekananda, Tagore, Aurobindo, and Gandhi himself played a significant part in shaping India's national identity and helping her to make a name and place for herself in the world. With the coming of independence and democratic self-government, new age groups have emerged for whom the nationalist struggle, in which Gandhi played so central a part, has become a history book happening or the memory of old men's youth. . . . The other-worldly concerns of Gandhian followers detract from the moral and material tasks of economic development and social mobility.[27]

The claim made at the beginning of this chapter, namely, that India's political independence was greatly dependent upon the renaissance-reformation of Hinduism, is upheld by scholarly investigations and conclusions such as the foregoing. But what of the present and the future? What is to be the relationship between the religion of Hindus and the political views and activities of Indians?

The example of Mahātma Gāndhī gives us a possible answer to our question. Deeply committed as he was to a religious way of life founded in the Hindu tradition as he interpreted it, and shaped in his religiousness by influences coming from outside that Hindu tradition, he was an outstanding, perhaps unique, pioneer in the application of religiously motivated belief and action to the realm of political problems. Now that those problems have been replaced by new ones, and the relevancy of the Gāndhīan beliefs and modes of activity are no longer so readily apparent, very few pay more than lip-service to the ideals and techniques that were so vital in bringing about a new Indian nation.

Ram Mohan Roy and the other seminal thinkers and doers of the past one hundred and fifty years each made their important contribution to the developing Indian-Hindu ethos and were then largely forgotten except on special occasions. Some more than others have left an observable working legacy, a continuation of their spirit through organized groups in the religious and political

[27] Lloyd I. and Susanne Hoeber Rudolph, *The Modernity of Tradition: Political Development in India* (Chicago, 1967), p. 216.

spheres—and those spheres are seldom, if ever, totally distinct. As to the future of the legacy of Mahātma Gāndhī, the so justifiably admired, great-souled saint of twentieth-century Hindu India, there appears to be little evidence that *religiously* this legacy will be more than one among a number of fairly equal contributors to a renewed assertion, existing at various levels of Hinduism since Ram Mohen Roy, that Hinduism has the resources to be and in fact is a religion with vitality and relevance for mankind in the twentieth century.

III

When we seek to evaluate the recent past of India and of Hinduism to discover, if possible, the primary currents and trends of the past century and a half, certain important matters stand out.

While it may be argued that no time in history is totally unique or different from all other times, there can be no question but that within this period Indian religion, culture, and society were collectively confronted by a convergence of external and internal forces that in their totality created conditions unlike anything that had been experienced before in the Indian subcontinent. The inrush of Western and basically foreign elements constituted in both its nature and its immensity something dynamically different from other invasions that had been experienced in the area since that of Alexander in the fourth century B.C.—or even, perhaps, since the Āryan invasion of the second millennium B.C. Westernization was not something that could be absorbed and quickly identified with Indian thought and ways. Unlike earlier foreign religious thought and custom—for example, that of the Parsis and Christians of earlier times—the incoming religous thought and practice was accompanied by equally foreign and equally dynamic political, social, and technological forces that combined with the different religious tradition to constitute a forceful opponent, rather than a supplicant seeking refuge within the Indian ethos.

During the period we have been considering, the events that took place were not simply a reenactment with different characters of the Muslim encroachment of previous centuries. The nineteenth century did not witness merely the arrival of a new political power concerned with political and economic exploitation, though that did happen; there was not only the importation and creation of another religious community of strikingly different beliefs and customs, though this occurred. What combined to make these new elements unlike their previous counterparts was their continued intimate association and identity with a powerful, irresistible non-Indian homeland and base. The invaders did not arrive and settle down peacefully in a new homeland. By their very nature, if not by intent, they demanded renovation of the area into which they had penetrated. And, the iconoclastic attitudes that they were expressing increasingly in their areas of origin demanded the right of expression, also, within the Indian context.

Further, we must take note of the obvious role of quick communication, and the means for the establishment of new identities which, while not absent previously, was now more readily available to certain groups and individuals. As many factors converged, avenues were opened for the emergence of a small number of individuals who would possess a mixture of the indigenous culture and its new opponent. It was and continues to be by these relatively few persons that the Indian-Hindu reaction to the Westernization/modernization confrontation is shaped and brought into active participation within present-day Indian society, culture, and religion. Some of these people are more Western than Indian, others ambivalent mixtures, and others primarily Indian but deeply cognizant of the nature and extent of the new elements, no longer foreign, demanding a place within the India of today.

Referring to the Western impact, Śrī Aurobindo declared that it

gave three needed impulses. It revived the dormant intellectual and critical impulse; it rehabilitated life and awakened the desire of new creation; it put the reviving Indian spirit face to face with novel conditions and ideals and the urgent necessity of understanding, assimilating and conquering them. The national mind turned a new eye on its past culture, reawoke to its sense and import, but also, at the same time, saw it in relation to modern knowledge and ideas. Out of this awakening vision and impulse the Indian renaissance is arising, and that must determine its future tendency.[28]

However, this necessary emphasis on the role of external impact upon India and its religious-cultural heritage must not be allowed to obscure the part that internal resources played, and continue to play, in reacting to that impact and creating the particular Hindu response. Professor Wilfred Cantwell Smith has reflected the thought of many students of religion in warning that undue emphasis upon outside, in this instance Western, impact is frequently a result of underestimation "of the dynamic, fluid quality of the so-called traditional religious systems." [29] Certainly the impact cannot be denied. Yet adequate understanding of contemporary Hinduism demands a clear appreciation that the Hindu response quickly produced a situation wherein Westernization and Indianization in the Hindu sphere were collectively engaged in a process more properly termed "modernization." Hinduism has been evolving throughout many centuries, sometimes almost imperceptibly but, nevertheless, evolving. Today it is more noticeably and dynamically engaged in that process than it was in most other periods of its history. Whether we term this "evolution," "modernization," or whatever, we should recognize it to be the characteristic essential to any tradition whose inner resources enable it and demand of it that it seek to be continually contemporaneous to its adherents.

The significant beginnings in thought and structure made by events and leaders of the past one hundred fifty years remain as the primary internal Hindu resources to be used in continuing modernizing trends in Indian life and Hindu religion. They, together with immediately present and future events, must be taken into account in the effort to understand Hinduism as, in company with other religions, it seeks to establish firmly its relevance for today and for the future.

[28] Sri Aurobindo, *The Renaissance in India* (Calcutta, 1946), p. 31 f.
[29] Wilfred Cantwell Smith, "Traditional Religions and Modern Culture," in *Proceedings of the XIth International Congress of the International Association for the History of Religions,* (2 vols., Leiden, 1968), I, 57.

CHAPTER THREE

HINDUISM AND
CONTEMPORARY
INDIAN YOUTH

Any human tradition or institution is highly dependent for its future upon the youth who share its locale and inherit its environment. All youth within the common society are future participants, active or inactive, in the tradition and its institutions. The importance of *educated* youth in this connection is obvious. They are most likely to be the shapers of the immediate future and the leaders of the larger mass that less consciously participates in the society and its surrounding culture. In a traditional society such as that of India, where mobility of status and opportunity for expression of leadership without education are severely limited, the role of educated youth is of primary significance.

There has been a general though not well documented impression in the West [1] that educated Asian youth are either in revolt against their traditional religions or, at least, very little concerned

---

[1] See, for example, Aileen D. Ross, *Student Unrest in India* (Montreal, 1969), pp. 150–57.

with them. This impression has been the result, in part, of a non-Asian conviction that the Asian religions are completely at odds with the modern scientific-technological world. Also, it is sometimes the product of contact with Asian youth who either are in revolt against the parental religion or who appear to be so eager to absorb modern knowledge that the observer mistakenly assumes that non-Western presuppositions are being forgotten or being cast aside.

The problem here involves not only determining whether there is a revolt against or lack of interest in religion; it also requires that where there appears to be rejection or indifference we ascertain what it is that is being discarded or ignored. Is it the folk religion and cult, the great tradition and the philosophical-theological presuppositions inherent to it, the specifically religious acts and social customs of the broad total tradition, or the general social structures and mores possibly peripheral to religion? Is it all of these, one of them, or a combination of some of them?

In the instance of India and Hindu youth it is of the utmost importance that a distinction also be made between those young people closely associated with the more Westernized large urban areas, and those whose background and present activity is more intimately related to the village and the less Westernized smaller urban areas. Both, if they are presently at the level of college and university study, represent the core from which future Indian Hindu leadership will come. The former, however, are more likely to have and to produce a greater number of culturally and religiously disaffected individuals. They more frequently come from parental backgrounds where this process has already been at work, and they are surrounded by an environment often adulterated and not typical of Indian culture or Hindu religion. Their intellectual and material resources set them off from their fellow Indians to the degree that they are less reliable as indicators of the broader mass of Indian youth, either uneducated or educated. Of course, they will have a very important role to play in the future of India and Hinduism. But whether conscious of it or not, like the late Jawaharlal Nehru, many could properly describe themselves as being at home in neither the East nor the West.[2]

While not free from many of the same problems of ambivalence, and subject also to forces that are not yet meaningfully indigenous, Hindu youth who come from the countryside and receive their initial higher education removed from the larger urban centers remain more intimately associated with traditional living Hinduism. Because of this our primary source for the following discussion is a study of students at a large "provincial" state university situated in a suburban town adjacent to a more tradition-oriented South Indian city.

I

Sometimes referred to as the "Brāhman University," the University of Andhra is located at Waltair near the industrial city of Visakhapatnam in the South Indian state of Andhra Pradesh. Following the English-Indian system of higher education, the university serves the state of Andhra as the degree-granting institution for constituent three-year colleges throughout the state, as well as being itself the residential graduate teaching and research institution. All resident students at the university possess at least the Indian Bachelor of Arts, the Bachelor of Science, or their equivalents. This means that they have had a minimum of eleven years of school and three years of college before entering the university. In American terms this is equal to having completed the first two years of college. All students work initially toward the master's degree or its equivalent. Those involved in our study were approximately equally divided between first- and second-year students in the normal two-year master's program. A few were in programs of study requiring more than two years' residence.

The selection of Andhra University as the site of our investigations was primarily the result of the conviction previously suggested, namely, that a modern university removed from a large, Western-

[2] Jawaharlal Nehru, *Toward Freedom* (New York, 1941), p. 353.

ized metropolitan area would furnish a more representative insight into contemporary educated young Hindus and their relationship to Hinduism. With very few exceptions, the students come from the villages and small towns of Andhra state; they received their early education in surroundings and forms similar to that experienced by their peers throughout India; and now in their university careers they retain a personal and cultural identity with their indigenous roots. They are not, of course, unchanged by their education; but they continue to be identified with the typical Indian life of today and return to it immediately they set foot beyond the university campus.

The study was made with the close collaboration of the Departments of Anthropology and Philosophy and with the enthusiastic cooperation of the university administration, faculty, and students. Graduate research scholars and faculty members aided in preparing a set of questions that on the basis of a trial run were reformulated for the final study. Care was taken not to ask questions in a sequence revealing a relationship between one general series and another, but to space them so that the individual's concern for consistency in his answers would not inhibit free and ready response. With the aid of the Department of Statistics of the university, a system of random sampling was followed in the selection of students to be interviewed, and care was taken to insure that adequate and proportional representation of the various areas of study was secured. No prior information concerning the caste background of the students could be obtained; this knowledge was only gained from the students themselves at the close of the interviews. Of the 204 students whose interviews were completed, 103 were members of caste groups falling within the upper three varṇa classifications, the so-called twice-born castes; [3] 91 were from the castes ranking within the Śūdra classification, the lowest varṇa group; and 10 re-

[3] See M. N. Srinivas, *Caste in Modern India* (Bombay, 1962), chapter 3, for a discussion of the problems in relating "varṇa" to "caste." "The *varṇa*-scheme refers at best only to the broad categories of the society and not its real and effective units. . . . The *varṇa*-model has produced a wrong and distorted image of caste," p. 65 f.

ferred to themselves as "Untouchables." [4] Upon the advice of faculty members and the students themselves, these three general categories and the sexes were used in tabulating the results of the interviews. The 204 interviewees were divided as follows:

	Twice-born Castes	Śūdras	Untouchables
Male	83	72	10
Female	20	19	—
	103	91	10

In an attempt to avoid any problems that might have arisen if the students had been interviewed by a non-Hindu Westerner, the primary interviewing and presentation of the questionnaires was done by two Hindu graduate research scholars, one in philosophy and one in anthropology. I myself talked with any of those interviewed who indicated they would like to talk with me, and conversed about the interviews with many students at random. The 204 students interviewed represented approximately 7 percent of the total student body; and the division of the sexes, by chance, was close to the proportional division within the university. No figures are available to indicate whether the general caste divisions approximate the caste proportions within the university, although faculty and students suggest that here, too, the random sampling came close to the caste background proportions.

The ages of the men interviewed range from 17 to 35, with 78 percent of them falling into the 20 to 24 age group. The median age of the men was 22. The women ranged in age from 18 to 28, 71 percent being in the 19 to 22 age group, with an overall median age of 21.

Fifty-eight percent of the men were in physical and biological sciences and engineering, 30 percent in the social sciences, and 11 percent in the humanities. Among the women 43 percent were in

[4] It is interesting to note that members of this group use this term when speaking in English to designate themselves. They and others found nothing repugnant or objectionable in the term itself, but rather in what it stood for, at least so they assured me. Members of this group were amused by my preference for terms such as "Harijan" or "non-caste people."

the social sciences, 36 percent in physical and biological sciences, and 20 percent in humanities, primarily languages. However, we found little if any differences among student answers to our questions that would indicate a relationship between fields of concentration and answers given to questions.

II

Our first concern was to determine the previous and present worship or cultic habits of the students. Almost half, 47 percent, said they regularly visited temples as children and while they lived at home. An almost equal number, 44 percent indicated that they did so only occasionally; and the remaining 8 percent said they never did. Only among the men of the twice-born group had over half (65 percent) attended temples regularly. The only marked deviation from the general pattern, perhaps not a surprising one, was that half of the Untouchables had never visited temples as children or while they were living at home.

When asked about their temple attendance since they had come to the university, approximately a fourth of the students (22 percent) replied that they went at least once a month. A slightly larger number (25 percent) went twice a month or more often, and among the remaining 50 percent there was an almost equal division among those reporting that they never went, rarely went, or attended only occasionally. Here, again the percentage of regular attendance on the part of the male members of the higher caste groups was the highest, with little drop from the childhood and home habits, and the patterns of the male Śūdras who had regularly attended temples in childhood and at home remained approximately the same. However, the total number who never attended increased from 17 to 35. Little or no change was present among the women; and now 8 rather than 5 of the Untouchables reported that they never entered a temple.

Reasons given for temple attendance both previously and currently most frequently stressed duty toward the god or gods involved, but did understandably acknowledge the role of the parents and family in the childhood patterns. Often in comparing earlier attendance with present behavior the statement was made, "As a child I followed my parents; now I know why I go. Now I want to go."

It is of interest that when the student returned home on vacation from the university there was little variation in behavior from when the student was on his own at the university, except that a few who rarely or never went while at the university said that at home they did go to satisfy the elders of their family.

The emphasis upon religious duty as the reason for temple attendance by respondents as university students and when returning home occurred when the questions were asked independently, with a third or more of the students (35 percent on attendance at the university, 42 percent on attendance at home) selecting the phrase, "By way of religious duty which is regularly discharged" as most correctly stating the motivation behind their attendance. In both instances—at home and at the university—"festive, recreational and social reasons" were cited by approximately a quarter of the students (19 percent when at home—26 percent when at the university) as the primary motivation. However, when asked in another context whether the reasons for going to the temple at the university were different from those for going at home in family surroundings, of the 149 answering affirmatively, 88 percent stated that "devotion to, or faith in God" was now the primary reason, with only a minimal number (5 percent) stressing "duty" or "festive, recreational and social reasons."

Of course, in all the foregoing there were many variables, individual patterns and changes, and personal motivations or lack thereof that cannot be presented without detailed consideration of each case. However, if the investigation is at all reliable, up to this point certain conclusions of a general nature appear to be valid. First, a little more than 90 percent of the students had visited temples regularly or occasionally as children. About two-thirds (62 percent) do so while away from home at the university, and a little over half (57 percent) go to a temple once a month or more frequently when they are home from the university.

Further, when specifically asked if their reasons for temple going are now different from when they were younger, the great majority no longer spoke of religious duty, or of the "festive and social" reasons which play a large role in the temple's traditional place in Hinduism, but rather emphasized personal religious devotion and spiritual faith. There is room here, obviously, for speculation about the awareness on the part of the students of a present need to justify something done previously without a totally free choice. There is also reason to conclude that growing social and intellectual maturity on their part is leading to an inner personalization and rationalization of accustomed actions.

As students of Hinduism are aware, a central feature of Hinduism, and one which binds together many local religious regions into larger cultic and sectarian areas, is the widespread custom of pilgrimage to important regional or India-wide temples or shrines. The students were asked whether they had visited any famous shrines, the names of those visited, approximately how long ago, and the reasons for the visits. Not counting the Untouchables, of whom only 3 had ever visited such temples, 90 percent had made at least one such pilgrimage. Approximately half of these had visited two or more shrines, with a number having gone to as many as four or five. Including 7 Untouchables, only 26 of the 204 students had not made at least one pilgrimage. Over one-third of the students (36 percent) had made a visit within the last twelve months.

In the list of the reasons for the pilgrimages, there were noticeable differences between the caste groupings and between the men and women. Of the twice-born men, 36 percent went as a "religious duty," while only 15 percent of the Śūdra males went for that reason; 65 percent of the higher-caste women and 47 percent of the Śūdra women gave that as the primary reason for their visits. Among the males of both these groups, around 27 to 28 percent went to "fulfill a vow," while of their female counterparts 10 percent gave this as their motivation. Between 15 and 18 percent of the men and a somewhat smaller percentage of the women listed participation in the prevalent Indian "educational tour" during college as the means and purpose of their visits. Less than 1 percent of the upper-caste men went to the shrines for "festive, recreational and social reasons," while over 23 percent of the Śūdra men went for these purposes.

A question that evoked answers frequently related to visits to important shrines was one concerning occasions when the student had made special prayers and vows to deities. Excluding the Untouchables, only one of whom had made such a prayer or vow, two out of three (67 percent) had. Of these over a third had done so within the past year. Sixty-two percent of all the students stated that the reason for their special prayer or vow was related to the passing of examinations or the obtaining of promotions, and one out of four (26 percent) listed personal or family illness as the reason. In a number of cases students cited vows made by their parents at the time of their birth, vows which they now had taken upon themselves as their own.

Most frequently, the vow and its fulfillment were related to the offering of a portion of the individual's hair to the deity at his shrine. Slightly over half (54 percent) made such an offering, while others fulfilled their vow by the visit itself or by making an offering of coconuts. One out of ten reported that their vows were fulfilled by the giving of money. Of course, hair and coconuts also have a monetary value to the temple.

An interesting insight into the students' attitudes toward temple visitation and the worship of images was furnished by their response to a question asking their opinion of people who frequently go to the temples. Over 56 percent thought such people to be "devout and good people worthy of emulation." Approximately 10 percent thought them to be "unwise people who deceive themselves," and 5 percent classified them as "clever people trying to deceive others by ostentatious show of piety." Five, or half, of the Untouchables considered such people to be "superstitious tradition followers."

When the religious backgrounds of the students were explored, it was discovered that in only 9 of the homes from which they came were no images of deities kept and worshipped. Of the parental homes 159 (78 percent) had at least one and more often many images that were worshipped daily, while 36 (18 percent) of the homes had images that were worshipped at least once a week. Caste differences were quite evident here in that 96 percent of the twice-born homes had images and worshipped them daily, while only 66 percent of the Śūdra homes did so. Of the Untouchable homes only one worshipped daily before images, 6 did so weekly, and 3 had no such images to worship.

In almost half (43 percent) of the homes, all members of the family participated in worship, with the remaining homes being divided equally between those where the worship was primarily by the mother or the women only and those where worship was limited chiefly to that done by the parents. Of course, most of these homes were the scenes of communal family living, and on special occasions all or the majority of members participated in the worship before the images. Only 2 of the students in whose homes there was worship reported that they themselves had never participated in the worship since they had become college students.

Attention was next turned to the prayer habits of the students themselves both before and since entering the university. Over two-thirds (70 percent) of the men reported that they had prayed frequently before coming to the university, and 90 percent of the women reported the same. The figures remained almost exactly the same after entering the university for all the women and for the men of the Śūdra classification, while 10 percent of the twice-born men dropped from the frequent category to that of rarely or never. Two of the Untouchables who previously had prayed frequently reported that now they never pray, making a total of 7 Untouchables in that category. Twenty percent of the Śūdras, a slight rise over the preuniversity figure, said they never pray now, while 5 percent or twice the previous number of the upper-caste males said they no longer pray.

A matter closely related to prayer habits is that of keeping images of deities in one's living quarters. Two-thirds (65 percent) of the students reported that they had one or more images of deities in their dormitory rooms. Frequently, they also mentioned figures of the Buddha, pictures of Christ, crosses, and pictures of national heroes such as Swāmī Vivekānanda and Mahātma Gāndhī whom they considered worthy of veneration if not worship. Five of the 10 Untouchables had no images, and 2 were careful to point out that they only had images of the Buddha before which they meditated but did not pray. Of all the students, 14 made a point of the fact that while they had images in their rooms, the prayer or silent meditation in which they engaged was not directed to the images; 136 reported that they did direct prayers to these images, with 106 doing it daily.

Obviously, ritual is central to religion and the society of which it is a part. This is particularly true of those acts termed "rites of passage" by students of society and religion. The more secular the society, the more these matters are taken care of by governmental or social services; in the more religiously oriented society, they are intimately related to religious sanction and religiously approved functionaries and procedures. Much of the basic strength of Hinduism, and the vivid evidence of its day-to-day presence among its adherents, is to be found in these rites. They are striking examples of the intimate relationship between religion and daily life wherein the participants find life enriched by the religious grounding and support furnished through the sacred act.

Initiation of the young male of the twice-born castes into full male religious and social status within the group through the investiture of the sacred thread (upanayana) is a primary instance of a Hindu rite of passage. By its very nature, among the students interviewed it was limited to the 83 men in the twice-born group. All these men stated that they had had or intended to have the ceremony. Fifty-three of them believed it essential that those qualified undergo it, while 24 did not consider it essential and 6 had no opinion. Among the women of this same general caste ranking, 12 thought it to be essential and 8 did not. Of the total group surveyed, the division between those who, whether themselves entitled to it or not, thought it essential and those who did not was about even. Of those holding it to be essential the great majority said they did so because it was one's duty to uphold tradition. Those considering it unessential gave numerous reasons, among them that "rituals have lost their meaning and serve no purpose," that "it upholds the evil of caste," and that "it is too difficult for a modern person to follow the demands that the ceremony places upon him." It is interesting that these negative opinions revealed no particular caste bias and were frequently given by students entitled to the ceremony.

Marriage, of course, is another central rite of passage within both the religious and the social context. For women in many aspects it has traditionally approximated the male upanayana in marking the moment of full acceptance into society. Of the 37 students already married, all but one had participated in a religious ritual rather than being married by civil registration. Three-fourths (74 percent) of all the students indicated a preference for a religious ritual at the time of marriage, while the remainder were about equally divided between preference for civil registration and lack of any strong opinion on the subject. The great majority of those who preferred a religious ritual held that it is a good tradition, makes a marriage sacred, and binds the couple together better than mere civil registration could do. Those stating a preference for civil registration emphasized the economic burden placed upon the family by the religious ritual and cited this as the reason for their choice of the inexpensive procedure of civil registration.

When asked whether they had or would perform death ceremonies in the traditional religious manner, all but 7 of the 204 answered in the affirmative. Sixty-nine percent believed that death ceremonies should be performed in this way and 27 percent did not, even though they evidently had performed or would perform them. Almost half of the students listed tradition as the reason for their affirmative answer, with a substantial group (17 percent) also citing the importance of the proper religious ceremony in insuring the "peace of the soul of the dead." The negative respondents placed their emphasis upon a lack of belief in religious rituals on their part and their conviction that such rituals were a "waste of time and money." It is interesting to note here that while there were a few students who were consistent in their deprecation of religious rituals, some who saw no value in such rituals at the time of death were firm believers in their value at the time of marriage. In other words, they were making a selection among traditional rites in the light of their judgment as to the value of the rite.

Turning from the specific area of religiously sanctioned status through a traditional rite of passage to the more general question of caste membership, 125 (61 percent) of the students stated that they did not believe "in the traditional divisions of Hindu society and the code of conduct ascribed to them according to tradition." Here, also, there were many possible variables that could only be revealed in individual conversations. Generally speaking, those who opposed caste did so on the grounds of its divisive role in Indian society. They emphasized their conviction that separate codes of conduct or areas of productive function within the society determined on the basis of birth were foolish and detrimental to India's development as a modern political economic state. They did not, however, give any indication of opposing caste distinctions in the matter of marriage, and some indicated approval of caste if it were reinterpreted to meet modern conditions.

It was in this matter of caste that the answers given by the various groups revealed the greatest differences. Slightly over half (56 percent) of the men in the twice-born group were in favor of traditional caste distinctions and functions, while only 5 percent of the women in that group held the same position. Two-thirds (67 percent) of the Śūdras were opposed to caste divisions and ascribed functions, as were 9 out of the 10 Untouchables. In private conversation many of the students declared that caste membership meant nothing to them in their relationships while at the university (perhaps too strong a declaration on their part), and that they were opposed to any caste distinctions except possibly in the realm of marriage. But they readily acknowledged that once beyond the confines of the university and back within the structures of the family, the village or town, and their occupations, their present "liberal" attitude toward caste would of necessity disappear. A frequent complaint was that unless they demonstrated complete caste loyalty, their hope of employment and social status commensurate with their abilities would be thwarted.

In a companion question about the practice of the four traditional stages of life (āśramas) in the modern world, 44 percent felt they should be practiced. The twice-born men in particular felt that the following of these stages—student, householder, hermit, and ascetic (sannyāsī)—was of importance in perpetuating the values of Hindu society as well as bringing spiritual fulfillment to the individuals involved. Two men and one woman had never heard of the āśramas. The Untouchables were unanimous in their rejection of them.

The surprising number of affirmative statements concerning the Āśramas was the most significant instance of evidence of a clinging to concepts of ideal action which were demonstrably not followed by the individuals and groups that signified their approval of such traditions.[5] Many who expressed highly critical views of traditional Hindu practice and belief frequently also expressed the conviction that a revival of ancient ideals and forms in modern guise was of supreme importance to the well-being of contemporary Hinduism.

A question that was included at the urging of the students themselves was whether the respondent believed family planning to be against the Hindu religious tradition. Over two-thirds (70 percent)

[5] See Edward Shils, *The Intellectual between Tradition and Modernity: The Indian Situation* (The Hague, 1961), p. 66.   Shils notes in regard to Indian intellectuals and the āśramas, "The third and fourth stages . . . continue to have tremendous power over those we interviewed."

indicated they did not think so, and 32 who did think it was contrary to Hinduism nevertheless intended to practice family planning when they were married. Here, as in many matters, there was little indication of caste differences of opinion.

Questions concerning vegetarian diet revealed that only a small number of the students were absolute vegetarians. However, only about a third (29 percent) said that they could reconcile themselves to eating beef, if circumstances necessitated it. Only 19 of the 103 students in the twice-born category said that they could imagine ever eating beef. A fair-sized group echoed the sentiments of one individual who remarked rather vehemently, "I prefer death to eating beef when eating beef is the only way to stay alive."

Astrology is a central feature of folk Hinduism that is not readily apparent to the Westerner who limits his study to the philosophical-theological tradition alone. Frequently accompanied by palmistry, it is found at most levels of Hindu practice, not at all excluding individuals in the higher echelons of Indian society. Sixty percent of the students affirmed their belief in astrology and/or palmistry. Only the Untouchable group had a majority that did not believe in them. Approximately half (53 percent) of the students said that they regularly or occasionally followed the weekly astrological forecasts that are so prominent in most Indian newspapers. Among this group there were a variety of answers to a question as to whether they found the forecasts reliable for themselves. Generally, they held that they were. Frequent private consultation of astrologers and palmists was a widespread practice among the 60 percent who believed in these arts, and they stressed the necessity of finding well-trained practitioners and supplying them with accurate, detailed personal data.

In an attempt to understand the students' formal training in religion, we asked them to list the religious literature in which they had received instruction, their ages when they received the instruction, and who instructed them. Twenty-nine of them had received no such instruction; only 19 had had any formal instruction in the Vedas and 20 in the Upaniṣads. One hundred thirty-eight had been instructed in the *Bhagavadgītā,* and 160 in the Epics. Twenty-six also listed the Bible as a religious work in which they had received formal instruction.

The age at which this instruction was received varied so greatly that no pattern was discernible. A surprising number did not receive any instruction until they were in their late teens. Prior to that time their knowledge came primarily from the informal telling of stories from the Epics and the Purāṇas by their elders. Also, there was little if any discernible pattern in the source of the formal instruction or study. Approximately 20 percent received instruction from their parents and grandparents, and almost half (40 percent) listed self-study as the source of their knowledge of Hindu religious literature.

When asked what religious books they now read, 76 said they read none, 53 read the *Gītā* (often daily for inspiration), 21 cited works by Vivekānanda and/or Gāndhī, and only 2 mentioned the Upaniṣads. Four of the Untouchables referred to writings on Buddhism by the late Untouchable leader, Dr. B. R. Ambedkar.

In a further attempt to discover the role of central themes from the great tradition, the students were questioned about saṁsāra and karma. Fifty-seven percent of all the students believed in saṁsāra, the cycle of transmigration of the soul, with over two-thirds of those in the twice-born group doing so. Only the Untouchables, with 6 out of the 10 answering negatively, had a majority who did not believe in this basic Hindu presupposition. In regard to karma, a basic distinction must be made between karma that is passed from one existence over to a later existence and karma that is passed from one moment of this life to another later time in this same life. The students wanted to make this distinction clear, with 56 percent believing in both types of karma, while a large number of those who did not believe in karma as something carrying over from one life to the next did hold that it is an active force in the successive stages of this present life.

While it had not occurred to me, faculty and student advisers suggested that while being questioned concerning karma, students should also be asked whether they believed in fate. Seventy-one percent answered in the affirmative, 11 percent more than had said they believed in astrology and palmistry and 15 percent more than had believed in karma that passes from one life to another. It was interesting to note the number of students who ascribed to fate their success or failure in examinations, in obtaining the proper wives or husbands, and in securing various material goods. Not only were failures despite hard work laid at the door of fate, but successes without endeavor were also thought to be the result of fate.

At the center of all Hindu thought and tradition, the term Dharma has a long history and a wide range of possible meanings. The ancient Sanskrit usage, the various refined and technical differentiations used by diverse thinkers and intellectual traditions—these have combined in popular thought to create an image of the individual and the society. Student definitions of Dharma were extremely diverse and often expressed in imprecise and immature ways. However, in one fashion or another they reflected the understanding of Dharma expressed by contemporary philosophers—for example, "the moral law as understood by man's reason and conscience and as found in the scriptures and interpreted by [the] Brahmanas" [6]—and by popular writers: "the general Hindu way of life with a religious sanction behind it." [7] The large majority of the students, in one fashion or another, were trying to express their belief that there is that which is proper in thought and action, and it has a transempirical or supramundane sanction.

When asked whether they believed the principles of Hindu Dharma to be applicable to their lives today, 85 percent said they did, while 8 percent said they did not know what the principles of Dharma are. In their statements as to why they believed the principles of Dharma to be applicable today, the students reflected the ancient teaching that non-Dharma (Adharma) could only result in social and cosmic chaos, as well as the firm conviction that

[6] K. Satchidananda Murty, *Indian Foreign Policy* (Calcutta 1964), p. 129.
[7] Nirad C. Chaudhuri, *The Intellectual in India* (New Delhi, 1967), p. 1.

moral law is founded in the very structure of man and the universe. The unsettled conditions of today are the inevitable result of lack of heed of Dharmic principles. And the students strongly felt that the hope for the future lies in the inculcation and practice of the principles of Dharma among the Hindu peoples.

Brief mention should be made of a question that produced results far different from those expected. As a Westerner whose knowledge of Hinduism was first founded upon aspects that were most closely associated with the great tradition of philosophical-theological thought, I was greatly interested in student response to a question as to the individual's conception of himself. It was thought that answers might reveal beliefs reflecting the absolute nondualism (Advaita) of Śaṅkara, the qualified nondualism (Viśiṣṭādvaita) of Rāmānuja, the dualism (Dvaita) of Madhva, etc. Whether the error of expectation was the result of my overestimation of the role of such sophisticated thought or the question itself was poorly presented, the result gave little if any indication that the students were conscious of these traditions when faced directly with the problem of who and what they as individuals really were. Few answers revealed a philosophical or religious sophistication that many of us in the West assume to be present in the educated Hindu. Most frequently the statement was made that "I am a student, a future engineer, etc."

We were also very much interested in ascertaining the attitudes and actions of the Hindu students in relation to other religions and their adherents. Over two-thirds (70 percent) indicated that they had personal friends who were not Hindus, and 90 percent of the students said they did or would dine with people who were not Hindus. However, the great majority of this group of 185 said that they eat with people of other religions only in public places and would not or could not do so in their own homes. Of those who do not or would not dine anyplace with non-Hindus, almost all noted strong disapproval by their parents of such practices.

A matter of particular interest in India today is the role of non-Hindu Indians in the political sphere. When questioned as to whether India should have a Muslim or Christian president and/or prime minister, 85 percent of the students answered that they considered the matter to be of no consequence. A few of those who answered negatively indicated that their attitude was directly related to what they considered to be the problem of Muslim loyalty to India so long as a declared Muslim religious state, namely Pakistan, was at India's borders. Despite antagonism toward Christian missionary activity revealed by other questions, Christian Indians were not, evidently, thought to be unworthy of high political office. Also, 87 percent of the students stated specifically that they did not believe the Hindu religion should influence Indian politics.[8] It should be noted here that some faculty members, when informed of the results of this aspect of the study, commented upon the widespread and determined effort of educated Indians to demonstrate publicly their support for a politically secular India, although they did not always follow this ideal at the grass-roots level of their own political activity.

A final question concerning the various religions in India, and one not unrelated to the role of religion in political activity, asked for opinions about freedom of religious propaganda and conversion. Over half (60 percent) of the students maintained that all religions should have such freedom. However, it was at this juncture that the most outspoken criticisms were made of the activities of Christian missions. It was not always clear whether this criticism was limited to the work of *foreign* Christian missionaries. There were comments indicating that most of the students make the same assumption as Indians in general, namely, that once indigenized and no longer under foreign domination, Indian Christianity will lose its converting zeal. Interestingly, 87 percent responded negatively to the question as to whether Hindus should convert all other Indians to Hinduism so that the country would have only one religion. While a large number seemed to feel the need for Hindu ideals and traditions as operative norms in contemporary Indian society, they were not at all anxious that religious pluralism be

[8] See chapter V for a consideration of this.

overcome. It is interesting to speculate as to whether they discern any difference between "Hindu ideals and tradition" in personal and social life as part of the shared inheritance of all Indians and the more specifically spiritual commitments that differ among the religions.

For me one of the most unexpected results of our study was elicited by the request that the students name the Hindu religious thinker(s) and/or leader(s) each admired most. Forty percent gave as their first or only choice Swāmī Vivekānanda, the founder and organizer of the Rāmakrishna Vedānta Society at the end of the nineteenth century. Many saw in him the proper, heroic attitude necessary on the part of Hindus today. Vivekānanda was praised as the man who gave Hindus a basis for pride in their own culture and tradition and, equally if not more importantly, demonstrated that Hindu religion had a message for all mankind. Many were convinced that the West, and America in particular, still vividly remembers the dramatic appearance of the dynamic swāmī before the Parliament of Religions at the Chicago World's Fair in 1893. The next most frequently mentioned names were those of Śaṅkara, Gāndhī, and Rāmakrishna, each being cited as the first or only choice by about 12 percent of the students.

The final specific question presented was a request that each individual list what he considered to be the major problem for Hinduism in twentieth-century India. One-fourth said they saw no problem, with the largest proportion of these among any one group being Untouchables. Also, more Śūdra men than twice-born men were unaware of major problems confronting contemporary Hinduism. As would be expected, the problems that were presented were of a varied nature. The most frequently mentioned cited in one way or another the poor religious propaganda and insufficient or inadequate religious instruction given children and young people. Eight percent listed the lack of sincere Hindu leaders and an equal number the work of Christian missionaries as being Hinduism's greatest problem. Only slightly over 3 percent mentioned the impact of science and/or the West. A general impression was given that little attention had been given to the problem, and that the question came as a surprise.

III

What conclusions may legitimately be drawn from the results of this study? Is it correct to assume that the religious attitudes and habits of the students interviewed reflect similar patterns on the part of their counterparts throughout India? Since we are concerned with modern trends in Hinduism we must of necessity move from the particular instance to the broader sphere if Hinduism and not the religion of a limited area or people within India is to be considered. While recognizing the possibility of being too sweeping in our conclusions, I do believe that we can correctly project the results of the Andhra survey into a broader all-India perspective.[9]

The first thing to note is that educated Indian youth have strong religious roots and generally remain firm in their relationships to those roots. Yet, it must be immediately stated that this religious grounding is more in the nature of unconsciously appropriated philosophical-theological presuppositions than it is carefully thought-out and developed intellectual affirmations. To expect the latter of any people not professionally engaged in religion would be unrealistic, of course; but the tendency in the West to assume that educated Indians are also educated as Hindus must be recognized as erroneous. The young Hindu of today is not carefully nurtured in the intellectual classics of his religious tradition; he is not taught the subtleties and philosophical nuances that are characteristic of the major branches of Hindu philosophy-theology; and he evidences little concern about learning of these in any structured, formal manner.

The nature of his religiousness is basically that of the Hindu people as a whole; that is, it is founded upon the inherited popular understandings of the "great tradition" of Hindu thought, in conjunction with the all-India and local myths and legends that form

[9] The possible differences suggested earlier between students in large metropolitan "Westernized" centers and those in the "provinces" should be remembered.

the base of popular mass Hinduism. The high level of education that separates him from the mass does enable him to separate the inherited "myth" from the more intellectual elements of Hinduism when he is called upon to do so; but in general his lack of precise knowledge of the latter and his own contentment with and feeling of support from his inherited cultic moorings lead him to continued participation in the level of religion that surrounded him in his childhood. His education, while primarily in subjects other than religion and philosophy, nevertheless serves to make him aware of the enduring qualities he considers to contain the essential spirit of Indian culture, which is identical to his mind with sophisticated Hindu religion. There is thus a combination of cult and dimly perceived intellectual affirmation, with the first now subject to cautious criticism where it is thought to be needed and the latter vehemently defended when it is questioned or attacked by others.

There is little evidence that modern education leads an appreciable group to a complete or meaningful break with their religion; if there is such a break it is from traditional cultic observances rather than from the inherited conceptions of the nature of man, existence, or the Divine. Further, there is a strong appreciation of tradition and the value it possesses in giving smooth continuity to life and to society. There is little indication of a determination to change existing patterns in personal, family, or community life; these have proved their worth in the past and are believed to be necessary for the present and the emerging future. They are not considered to be in essential opposition to the new forms of larger social life and economic structure that are emerging as the disparate and provincial subcontinent is working toward becoming a unified nation-state. Indeed, the existing patterns are held to be necessary for the viable incorporation of any new forms; they constitute the modality essential for the preservation of the Hindu way of life. Any future that will escape the chaos prevalent among other nations must rest upon these Hindu understandings of existence and the Hindu values they perpetuate.

CHAPTER FOUR

POPULAR ESOTERIC
RELIGION:
RĀDHĀ SOĀMĪ SATSAṄG

In the general Western mind it is thought that much of Indian religion is centered around the possession of secret knowledge, of an
"esoteric" teaching limited to a few uniquely endowed or instructed
individuals. It is frequently forgotten that because any such tradition or movement is esoteric, and therefore limited to the relatively
few who are initiated, in cannot be typical and is not possessed by
the masses in a large historic religion.

Nevertheless, it is true that throughout Indian religion there has
been and is a strong element that is esoteric in nature. The great tradition in its various expressions has supported the concept of the
special knowledge or condition necessary for release (mokṣa) from
the round of karmic existence. Despite the fact that in theory such
knowledge may be open to anyone, its attainment is extremely difficult and it is seldom won. In the realm of the folk religion of India
this same element has been present, frequently in a more meaningful fashion. Supported in his belief both by the great tradition and

by the mythic-legendary basis of his daily religious piety and cult, the Hindu has firmly believed that there are those "holy" persons who possess the means for man to overcome his karmic limitations. Often these specially endowed individuals are understood to be helpers in the attainment of specific goals within the realm of saṁsāra; sometimes they are considered to be much more than that, for they are believed to be "divine" carriers of the key or knowledge whereby all limitations are overcome and karmic existence is erased forever.

The tradition of the ṛsis or seers who received the divine knowledge embodied in the Vedas, the sacred priests whose secret knowledge was essential to the performing of the sacrifices necessary to uphold human society and the very universe itself, the wise ācāryas, teachers, whose eternal wisdom is to be discovered in the Upaniṣads and other commentaries upon the Vedas, the holy and divine men and women remembered through epics and legends, the more local saints renowned for their indifference to and victory over human limitations—all these and more from Hindu history continue to contribute to the firm place in Hinduism held by the search for hidden truth that when known brings release. The hero of traditional India has been the saint, the holy man, the God-man who, beyond possessing freedom for himself, makes it available to others. Today, the rise of new national political heroes and the remembering of some past ones like Śivājī have not yet intruded upon the preeminent place accorded to the holy teacher, the guru whose knowledge is the ultimate *summum bonum*.[1]

The central position of the holy person in both intellectual and popular Hinduism has been strengthened by the corresponding place accorded to similar persons by other religions associated with Indian history. Jainism, Buddhism, and Sikhism have contributed their own holy heroes, and Islam through its Sūfī mystic tradition has furnished further examples of those who by "secret" paths gained the ultimate wisdom that equals salvation. All this has resulted in a

---

[1] See J. Gonda, *Change and Continuity in Indian Religion* (The Hague, 1965), chapter VIII, for a discussion of the place and role of the guru in traditional and contemporary Hinduism.

particular reverence for, if not worship of, the person believed to be a "jīvan-mukta," a freed soul now living in the midst of others still ensnared by their karmic past.

Contemporary Hinduism continues this intense concern for the holy person and his or her knowledge. While we must not make the error of assuming that all or most Hindus consider themselves to be active seekers after such persons and their knowledge, nevertheless the ideal is present within the fabric of modern Hinduism as a constant informing and invigorating factor. The ideal is not limited to some example from the distant legendary past; it is vividly present in the fresh memory of such figures as Rāmakrishna Paramahaṃsa and Śrī Aurobindo. While the great bulk of cultic Hinduism and personal religious devotion continues as it has for centuries and relatively few Hindu intellectuals still concern themselves with the subtleties of Hindu philosophy-theology, both these currents of traditional Hinduism are joined by another element that has been integral over the centuries—the sect gathered around the holy person.

These persons and their adherents, different as they often are, frequently are recognized as part of a long tradition that gives them an authenticity which would not be so easily accorded to persons or teachings not so grounded. While the holy person attains status in his or her own right on the basis of spiritual accomplishment, often that high status is conceived to be the inevitable continuation in the mundane sphere of a supramundane knowledge that has resided in the present incumbent's predecessors. Firmly committed to the belief that this knowledge is eternal and unchanging, and that it has been present in the empirical realm at least since the appearance of the Vedas, Hinduism does not consider the possessor of such knowledge to have anything essentially new. Since time immemorial there have been those few individuals who have possessed it and those even fewer persons who have imparted its riches to others.

As a result of this conviction, the nature and content of the knowledge or formulae resulting in release have not been as different, secret, or hidden as might be imagined. This is not to suggest that at the highest levels of attainment or initiation within a particular sect barriers are not present for all but the most select. But the general themes of belief, the procedures for spiritual development, and the nature of the reward or condition attained are similar, and frequently identical. Sects are seldom absolutely exclusive in the tradition to which they appeal and are often open in their recognition of other claimants to the knowledge necessary for release.

Especially since the time of the so-called Medieval Mystics and their Vaiṣṇava "bhakti" faith, this openness to a broad tradition of "holy knowledge" has produced in many groups a succession of widely famed and more locally known gurus believed by their adherents to be possessors and revealers of the ultimate knowledge. Often conceived as being in a line of direct succession one from another, they shared in a common despository of belief that has been adopted by later successors, sometimes varying greatly from the original teachings of their illustrious predecessors.

In North India the Sūfī tradition of Islam has been an additional unifying element among many such sectarian groups. This inheritance with its emphasis upon the man or woman of God who attains the point of the beatific vision of, if not immersion into, the Divine, was an important element in the religious fervor associated with Kabīr, and with Nānak and the founding of Sikhism in the fifteenth century. The end result of this eclectic combination of the themes of philosophic Hinduism with Vaiṣṇava bhakti and Muslim mysticism was the creation in North India of a religious atmosphere common to popular mass Hinduism and Sikhism. The movement we are now going to consider is, in some measure, the product of this eclectic combination.

I

The Rādhā Soāmī Satsaṅg (True Association of the Lord of the Soul) of Beas, near Amritsar in the Panjāb, is in some ways typical of the popular esoteric sect of today. It is atypical, perhaps, in the width of its appeal to Indians and non-Indians alike, but even here it is an example of the attraction that such forms of Indian religion frequently have today beyond the borders of India. Some readers may criticize my selection of the group and with good reason raise a question as to whether it is Hindu or not. The obvious fact that, in its teachings and in its cult, it is far removed from usually accepted definition of Hindu orthodoxy, and that its inheritance is Muslim and Sikh as well as Hindu, would seem to remove the Rādhā Soāmī from a discussion of contemporary Hinduism. However, it is just because of this quasi-Hindu nature and eclectic inheritance that it and sects like it must be brought to our attention if we seek to understand twentieth-century Hinduism. It is of the very nature of Hinduism to include and, indeed, to father such sectarian movements. The strictly orthodox Hindu may well deny the legitimacy of the relationship, and protest that such groups are not Hindu in any meaningful sense of the term as he understands it. But if this be true, then much of what has passed as part of Hinduism and Indian culture through the centuries must be declared to be non-Hindu. Such a subtraction would leave a Hinduism that has never existed except, perhaps, in the minds of a few—a religion much less typical of general Indian religion than the sectarian movements themselves.

As we shall see, the Rādhā Soāmī participates in the fundamental themes at the core of the great philosophical-theological tradition of Hinduism. It shares in the conviction of that tradition and of folk Hinduism that holy men come to the physical world with the purpose of leading mankind out of karmic bondage. It equals other groups in Hinduism in the vehemence of its protest against the religious exclusivism of non-Hindu religions. It appeals, though not exclusively, to the Indian religious traditions of the past that are part and parcel of Hindu history, and it expresses itself in the language of the Hindu spirituality which is its parent. Very importantly, in company with other Hindu religious groups of today, it is not averse to the use of meaningful religious language whatever its origin, Hindu or non-Hindu, Eastern or Western. And it is significant that as a sect also engaged in activities outside India, it possesses the qualities Louis Renou has suggested as necessary for such groups in that it is a "direct reflection from genuinely Indian forms of thought and spirit conceived and expressed by Indians." [2]

Briefly, the history of the Rādhā Soāmī Satsaṅg may be divided into two main parts. The early movement resulted from the spiritual genius of Shiv Dayal Singh of Agra in Uttar Pradesh, who formally founded the group in 1861 and became known as Soāmijī Mahārāj. Since his death in 1878, a succession of leaders or "Masters" has developed a colony of people in an āśram at Dayālbāgh (Garden of the Merciful) just outside Agra.[3] A number of followers are to be found throughout India, though at the present time the Rādhā Soāmī Satsaṅg of Dayālbāgh is not in a condition of great spiritual vitality, either at its central headquarters in Agra or in its regional local groups. Its Dayālbāgh center is known throughout India for its educational and welfare institutions, much more than for its religious teaching or impact on either the educated or the masses of the Indian people.

That aspect of the movement with which we are concerned is the Rādhā Soāmī Satsaṅg of Beas in the Panjāb. In 1856 a young Panjābī of Sikh background had in the course of his religious searching come under the influence of Soāmijī Mahārāj in Agra. He soon considered himself to be the chosen disciple of the Agra Master with the divine appointment to spread the Rādhā Soāmī faith into the Panjāb. Upon his retirement from the Indian army, this man, Jaimal Singh, founded an āśram in 1891 along the banks of the Beas river, where today a large colony is spiritually and physically vigorous in spreading its teachings both locally and throughout India.

The subsequent history of the colony at Beas centers around the person of Baba Sawan Singh Ji, also known as Huzur Mahārāj Sawan Singh, who as Jaimal Singh's immediate successor took over the leadership of the movement upon the death of the first Master in 1903. By all acounts a person of high intellectual powers, charismatic

---

[2] Louis Renou, *The Nature of Hinduism*, trans. by Patrick Evans (New York, 1962), p. 144.

[3] For a discussion of the early Satsaṅg at Agra see J. N. Farquhar, *Modern Religious Movements in India* (New York, 1915), pp. 157–73.

qualities of leadership, and sincere and deep spiritual resources, he has since become known as the Great Master. During the forty-five years of his leadership before his death in 1948, he succeeded in strengthening the physical condition of the colony at Beas and, more importantly, made more explicit the formal structure of religious thought and practice upon which the present movement rests.

He frequently toured throughout the Panjāb, where his preaching and teaching attracted many into the Satsaṅg. Local centers and halls for group meetings (satsaṅgs) were soon to be found in many of the cities and villages of the Panjāb and, as his tours became more widespread, in other areas of North India. However, the spiritual and physical center of the group continued to be at the Dera, as the colony at Beas is called. Everything within the Rādhā Soāmī group centers around the living Master, and since the colony at Beas is his home, it is not too great an exaggeration to refer to it as the Mecca or Rome of the movement. For the adherents of the Master at Beas the present leadership at Dayālbāgh in Agra is of no significance. For them the truth, the secret knowledge given by Soāmijī Mahārāj of Agra to Jaimal Singh, is now most clearly to be found in the succession of Masters at Beas.

Upon the death of Huzūr Mahārāj Sawan Singh, the leadership of the Rādhā Soāmī's passed to Sardar Bahadur Jagat Singh, an elderly disciple who had been a college professor of chemistry. Our information about each of the Masters is limited to sources within the Satsaṅg itself, with the result that we are presented in each case with the figure of a kindly, saintly, spiritual man of great powers. This is true in the case of Sardar Bahadur Jagat Singh and his short three and a half years of leadership before his death, though there can be no doubt that he was greatly overshadowed by the towering figure of the Great Master whom he succeeded.

His successor and the present Master, Charan Singh, is a grandson of the Great Master who before becoming Master in 1951 was a lawyer in Sikanderpur in the Panjāb. Born in 1916, a man of great physical and personal charm even to non-Satsaṅgis and now at the height of his intellectual and spiritual powers, he is obviously a worthy successor to the Great Master. As I can testify from personal conversation with him and by observation of him in the midst of his devout adherents, the leadership of an Indian religious sect such as the Rādhā Soāmī Satsaṅg of Beas does not fall upon men who are charlatans or insincere, as some people in the West might suspect. Penetrating through the fervent adulation and worship of his followers and the supporting atmosphere of the colony, the objective nonadherent must admit to being in the presence of a highly gifted and spiritually sensitive leader. Whatever be our attitude toward the teachings, members, and leadership of such groups, we will miss comprehending the genius and the strength of these integral aspects of modern Hinduism if we dismiss them as being anything less than sincere spiritual-religious teachings and movements grounded within the general Indian religious tradition.

II

As we have suggested, the central element around which sectarian Hinduism revolves is the holy person, man or woman, who possesses the knowledge necessary to overcome the karmic limitations that now circumscribe human beings. And fundamental to this belief in the ultimate value of that possessed by the person is the equally central conception that the knowledge and its possessor are *one*. The holy person, in essence, is not something distinct from the Ultimate Wisdom he or she possesses. The person is merely the present physical embodiment, incarnation, of the Ultimate Wisdom Itself. He or she is the means to Ultimate Knowledge which is identical with Ultimate Being, and at the same time *is* Ultimate Knowledge or Being. Speaking theologically, the epistemological means and the ontological end are ultimately one and the same. This, of course, is not something that is limited to Indian tradition. However, it is made vivid by the conviction of Hindu sects of this type that concrete embodiments of Ultimate Being are present now in the world of limited empirical being. The Rādhā Soāmi Satsaṅg finds its *raison d'être* in the actual physical presence of just such a person.

In Rādhā Soāmī terminology, the Master is a *Sat Guru,* the true (sat) teacher (guru) or giver of light.[4] The Master is the instrument whereby the Supreme Ruler, the Ultimate, comes into contact with the realm of humanity. A Sat Guru (sometimes the English term "saint" or Sanskrit-Hindi "saṅt" is used) has been brought into human existence to give initation (nām) and to lead properly prepared persons back to their true home, the highest spiritual region (Sach Khand). Such a Master is known as a "supreme saint" (Param Saṅt) if he is believed to have advanced to the highest possible level, that of the region of pure spirit.

Rādhā Soāmī writings about an individual Master, or the role and nature of Masters in general, are filled with ecstatic, adoring phrases to the point where the nonadherent feels he is entering a never-never land. However, underneath the excessively adoring, sometimes fanciful, verbiage a clear image emerges. A genuine Master is a combination of physical grace, intellectual wisdom, and personal humility. In his person and his activity he is the example of what the human person should and can be. He is not an ascetic and does not teach the necessity or even desirability of physical austerities, a point where the Rādhā Soāmī view is different from that of some other Hindu groups. Also, the Master is usually a person with family ties and business or occupational reponsibilities. It is one of the fundamental signs of a true Master that he accepts the normal responsibilities of human life and, most especially, that he furnishes his own livelihood and is not dependent upon others for his physical support. And, like all men, the Master participates in the common physical experiences of birth, pain, pleasure, and death.

However, all that we have just said is but a beginning and totally inadequate description of the Master; it is only the statement of the Master's obvious participation in human limitations and his purposive attainment of oneness with men. All this is but an outer cover, a façade that is meaningful because it embodies the Sat Guru so

---

[4] The following discussion is dependent upon the many publications of the group and personal conversations with Rādhā Soāmīs at the Dehra in Beas. See particularly Julian P. Johnson, *The Path of the Masters* (rev. ed., Beas, 1965).

that men may know, understand, and love him in ways that are meaningful to human beings. But the Master is so much more than this—in fact, ultimately so unlike this that the normal human descriptions are, finally, inadequate and in reality misleading.

Beyond possessing all the virtues idealized by humanity, the Master is the Ultimate, the Divine. He transcends all the limitations of the material, of man and the physical universe. He operates, as it were, in the infinite dimensions beyond time and space. Such dimensions are his home as well as the earthly sphere in which mere mortals come to know him. Above and beyond all that we know as men there are infinite planes of existence, worlds immense in their beauty which are open to the Master whom we see and hear on the limited earth. Since ultimately there is no difference between the Master we know and the Supreme or Ultimate Being, in the person of the Master standing before us we have the Absolute, the Ultimate, available to us. Except for the physical limitations that he has assumed for the purpose of his teaching-redeeming role, and which he can shed and reassume at any moment, there is nothing to distinguish the Master from the Ultimate Supreme One.

In his physical embodiment each Master has a specific time limitation in which to accomplish his mission. When the particular mission of a specific Master is finished, he purposefully leaves his body and turns his responsibility over to his chosen successor. The Master, now, is not dead in the sense that he has ceased to be. He has merely left his former dimension with its close contact with humanity to operate in the higher spheres of being that are always open to him. In his time here on earth he has embodied Ultimate Truth and made it available to man; now this work is to be done by others who actually are not other than he but are only different physical, worldly manifestations of the same Absolute Truth.

If we seek to understand the nature and functions of the Masters in a logical manner, it becomes obvious that there must be a structure of being, a plane or planes of existence behind or supporting the empirical world we know and in which the physically embodied Masters perform their work. It is the Rādhā Soāmī position that, yond the physical universe in a spatial sense; it is not measurably different in a physical, quantitative manner. One dimension of existence is separated from another dimension in this scheme of things by etherial qualities, by a greater amount of spirit and its resulting activity.

In this second sphere there are many planes or areas best described in human terms as heavens, purgatories, etc., with innumerable forms of life wherein character is rebuilt. Here many of the people of the earth go when they die. This is the dimension where the "astral plane" is to be found, the area that except for the purgative-reformatory regions is composed of a luminous light far beyond the comprehension of human beings. It is a realm in which spirit and matter are present in more equal amounts.

The third grand division (Brahmanda) is composed primarily of spirit, but there still remains an element of matter, though it is now highly refined. According to Rādhā Soāmī thought, this area and its ruler, Brahm, were mistaken by the ancient Hindu ṛsis for the Ultimate and Supreme. The Rādhā Soāmī Masters know, rather, that it is at one remove from the Absolute, and this knowledge is a part of the supreme knowledge which places them in a higher order than many of their ancient predecessors. In this third region the highly refined matter which remains is best described as mind; for mind, as distinct from spirit, is the supreme form of matter. Nevertheless, the continuing presence of matter, even in its most highly refined state as mind, is the continuation of a condition, a limiting karmic modification that prevents perfection.

The logic of this scheme to this point indicates what is to be expected at the fourth and most perfect division of being. This is the realm of Universal Spirit, the country of the Real (Sat Desh), the of Truth, of Ultimate Reality. Within its various subdivisions are an infinite number of souls free from all materiality. This realm of perfection, and there are no human words to describe. All that can be conveyed to the human mind is that here the dimension of the Universal Spirit is the seat of the Absolute of all that is. Like the previous supramundane spheres, only

like the Buddha, the Master's primary concern is to liberate
from this world of being. The Masters know the nature c
beginning of things and the structure of existence or being t
the finite, but even for them it is extremely difficult to conv
knowledge to the limited human mind. Knowledge of these
in a final manner is available only to the prepared and duly
person. However, in their graciousness the Masters hav
something of the nature of the totality of existence in
prehensible to the finite human mind.

The totality of being comprising all universes may
as falling into four main divisions.[5] Each differs from
the nature of the substances which compose it ar
phenomena to be found within it. Starting at the bot
physical universe (pinda) we know, there is the
matter mixed with a very limited amount of me
stuff. It is the mental and spiritual that give life
physical universe. Matter in itself is an inert
spirit, which serves as the self-acting essence
Ultimately, however, there is no such thing as
present. The Rādhā Soāmīs seem to suggest t
depleted form of spirit, a kind of spirit resid
spiritual state that it exists but no longer app
was.

Just above this universe composed pr
formed, as it were, by spirit, there is a
material substance is finer in structure
much more noticeable through its vib
or extent of the boundaries of spirit is
in all this that human words and con
misleading. This realm of being, fc

[5] Here again, I am almost exclusively dep
much that is written here is a paraphras
no written sources for these subjects oth
self, and Rādhā Soāmīs generally consi
tion. Katherine Wason, The Living Mc
into the adoration and love of the dev

more so, all description of it is fanciful and, ultimately, totally inadequate. There is no substitute for the soul's experience of it.

Fundamental to the foregoing conception of the structure of all existence, material and spiritual, is the belief in a similarly structured hierarchy of beings who are the rulers and directors of these spheres and their subdivisions. This "Grand Hierarchy," as it is called, is composed of the souls that have been selected by the Supreme One to serve as the governors of their assigned regions. When the Supreme One desired to bring existence into being, he created as his first individual manifestation a new center of being with its Lord (Agam Purush), and all subsequent areas of existence were the results of the Supreme Creative Energy brought into focus through this first region and its Lord. Creative energy has its origin in the Supreme, and now its diffusion is through the channel of the Grand Hierarchy of divine beings that emanate out from the source of energy and its prior manifestations. The result is an infinite number of planes or worlds of being each with innumerable lords and sublords.

For our purposes, and the purposes of the Rādhā Soāmī adherents also, the various members of the Grand Hierarchy are not of great importance. What is of central significance is the belief that the Great Masters (now best exemplified by the Masters of the Rādhā Soāmī Satsaṅg) work under the direct orders of the ruler (Sat Purush) of the fourth dimension of existence, the perfect realm of the Supreme and Universal Spirit. All members of the Grand Hierarchy may properly be thought of as gods, if it is clear that one means that they are possessors of powers and types of authority given to them by the Supreme Universal Spirit. But, more correctly, the members of the Grand Hierarchy are simply individual manifestations of the Supreme, and the Masters are supreme instances of such manifestations.

One additional element must be brought in at this point to complete the picture of the realms of being and the Grand Hierarchy. This is the existence of the "Negative Power" (Kal Niranjan), the supreme agent of creation and power in the region furtherest removed from the pure spirit. It is this creative power that is predominant in the first or world dimension of which we spoke earlier. It is this power, god if you want, with which men in their present condition must struggle. It is his responsibility to endeavor to hold the soul or spirit in the grip of the unrefined karmic infused matter that is fundamental to the human condition. He is the one who is charged by the Supreme Spirit with educating us in the elementary steps that are necessary before we can receive the more advanced lessons brought by the Masters. And this he does by imposing upon us the "laws of nature," the physical and material restrictions that frustrate the soul in its search for its full spiritual stature.

III

The foregoing outline of the nature of existence and of the powers that rule it presents the arena within which human beings live this and their many other lives. It is already quite evident that man as now constituted is conceived to be in some measure a combination of the material and the spiritual. Students of neoplatonism will be well aware of the similarities of thought and expression between the teachings of the third-century Master and that of the Rādhā Soāmī Masters of today. All who are familiar with the so-termed Perennial Philosophy, under whatever name it may have been presented before, will have been hearing familiar conceptions, and without further knowledge of Rādhā Soāmī teaching would be able to present the Rādhā Soāmī understanding of the structure and nature of man in terms not greatly different from those used by the Rādhā Soāmī Masters.

This similarity, perhaps identity, with other conceptions of the structure of existence is not an embarrassment to the Rādhā Soāmīs; rather, it is something that they gladly acknowledge. In company with other religious groups of this type, they maintain that Masters or messengers of the Truth have existed throughout time. Their cosmogony and their cosmology support this belief— in fact, demand it. Differences in terminology from one teaching or time to another are easily dismissed, and minor differences in content may be explained by the changing conditions of man or society. Similarities marred by significant differences are seen as evidence of the existence of false or pseudo-Masters who were, at best, only at the beginning stages of Truth.

The Rādhā Soāmī view of man is that he is composed of five parts. Man is, obviously, composed of physical body (Asthus Sharir). In addition, there is a finer inner body, a subtle or light body (Nuri Sarup), frequently termed the "astral body" in similar systems of thought. It is this part of the human being that enables man to make contact with the physical body and the outside world of being. With the death of the physical body it is this element or part of man that continues and is the means of expression for the individual in the higher regions to which he may go.

The third part of man is the causal body (Karan Sharir), which is the source of all that takes place in the life of the individual. It functions as the means of communication between the mind and soul, and between the mind and the astral body. In its realm reside the conscious and unconscious memories of all previous actions and existences of the individual, and it is from these that the particular character of the person is formed. It is the instrument of action and the mediator between the soul and the lower forms or aspects of the body that we have mentioned previously. Being higher in the scale of real being, it possesses more light and power, and while not free from matter is not completely bound by it.

The fourth part is the mind. Similar to, and easily confused with, the causal body, it is of a more subtle nature, more powerful and closer to the soul of man. However, there appears to be little difference between the two as they are described in Rādhā Soāmī literature. Both are necessary parts of man in any material dimension, and along with the subtle or astral body are essential aspects of man until he reaches higher regions of existence where they are no longer needed. It is only when man comes to "know" himself as pure spirit, knows by direct perception without extraneous faculties associated with empirical knowledge, it is only then that these normally essential parts of himself become unessential and nonidentifiable with the self.

Finally, there is the ultimate essence, the true being of man, the soul or spirit. All previously mentioned parts are but servants or instrumentalities of the soul; elements to be progressively discarded as the soul attains greater freedom from the matter that predominates in the lower dimensions of being. The soul (Purush, sometimes also called by the equally prevalent term Ātman), is a "spark from the Infinite Light," a derivative of the Supreme Spirit, and is one or identical with that Spirit in substance and qualities. It is true man, the Rādhā Soāmī say, though it would seem to be more precise to say that it is the essence or focal point around which the less and less fine, or more and more gross, elements of matter collect to constitute the being we designate as man.

The Rādhā Soāmī system presents a psychology of man that is not unfamiliar to students of classical Hinduism, Jainism, and Buddhism, not to mention a number of non-Indian systems of theology and philosophy. Here, again, we are quickly reminded of neoplatonism. There are four division (antashkarans) of the mind; manas, whose chief function is taste or feeling, chitta, which is the faculty of reasoning; buddhi, the intellect proper which discriminates; and, ahankar, the executive faculty and the awareness of individuality. In company with these faculties there are five passions, each destructive in nature. When the faculties are out of balance in their relation to each other, or when any one of them becomes perverted from its proper activity and attachments, the passions are individually or collectively more free to express themselves beyond even their normally unhealthy manner and become rampantly destructive.

Given the foregoing understanding of the constituent material and pyschological aspects of man, once the seeker on the Rādhā Soāmī path has made the all-important initial step of submitting himself to the living Master, his first concern must be with his mind. Neither moral nor immoral in itself, the mind is like a machine that follows the routine set for it by forces outside itself. The seeker of Truth must come to recognize that his mind in itself is simply an automatic responsive agent, and that basically it is matter, though of a highly refined sort. There is only one force that can ultimately bring about a change in the mind's routine attachments to the grosser materiality that surrounds it in human life, and that is a power that comes through and from the Master. Good and wise teachings in themselves are not powerful or persuasive enough to bring the mind to the point where it is able to free itself from its basic material nature. A thing cannot change itself qualitatively to such a degree that it ceases to be itself. It is necessary that something from outside be at work accentuating the desired qualities and their powers, but qualities cannot undergo changes which destroy them essentially. It is for this reason that the individual must cease being a person who follows his own mind (a manmukh), and become one who follows the guru (a gurumukh). Now he is no longer a slave to his mind and its material attachments; he is freed by the love and guidance of the guru. The previous master, his mind, has been superseded and put in its correct place by the presence of a new and proper Master, the living Master who is the embodiment of Supreme Truth.

A frequent concept in such systems of thought, and one fundamental to Rādhā Soāmī belief, is the conviction that there is a structural relationship between all existence and individual men. Man is a microcosm of the macrocosm that is the totality of existence. All levels of being are present in miniature in man, and because of this man can potentially communicate with all levels of being. If under the guidance of a true guru man develops the ability to go within himself, into these small replicas of the constituent parts of the larger whole, he will achieve identity with the infinite universes that are not only reflected there but are actually present within him.

The method for retreating into oneself, as taught by the Rādhā Soāmī Masters, reflects aspects of traditional Hindu yoga; and the means of describing the discipline and expressing its results reproduce language common to the mystic traditions of many religious cultures. While recognizing the presence in man of a number of "microcosmic centers" (chakras, "wheels"), Rādhā Soāmī concentrates its attention upon the "third eye" (tisra til), believed to be located between the eyes at the lower part of the forehead. The Masters teach that all concentration should be directed at this seat of the soul (also called Shivanetra, the eye of Śiva), and that there is no need to concern oneself with the other centers, since they are related only to levels of being below that of the Supreme Spirit.

By concentrating attention upon the third eye and, as a result, withdrawing from the outer world, one comes to a point where one's attention is all within oneself. The mind and the soul gather themselves together, as it were, and achieve some release from the material world that is their focus when they are in their usual human state. Now, while within himself, the individual has open before him the totality of being microcosmically present within himself. He has contact with all levels of existence; in fact, bècause he himself partakes of their essence, he is one with them all. There is now a recognition of the Truth, a participation in the "secret knowledge" taught by the ancient Masters in the Upaniṣads, namely, *tat tvam asi,* "Thou art that." Every person in his ultimate soul, separated from the various levels of material being, is the Supreme One. Man is essentially identical in substance with the Ultimate. This is the Truth he seeks; and in itself it is not a knowledge concerning a condition he may attain, nor is it only a knowledge of what he now is. Rather, it is a point where the knowledge, the truth, and the condition are recognized as being One.

One further essential feature of Rādhā Soāmī teaching must be mentioned. It, the absolutely indispensable role of the Masters, the centrality of the third eye, and the existence of the various dimensions of being with their Grand Hierarchy of rulers—all these combine to constitute the core of the "teachings of the Saints" (Santon Ki Siksha). This is the belief in the "Audible Life Stream," which Johnson designates as "the central fact in the Science of the Masters . . . the keystone of the arch . . . the cornerstone of the structure . . . the structure itself." [6]

Many words or terms are used in Rādhā Soāmī writings and conversation to refer to the Audible Life Stream. It is the "great spiritual Current," the Shabd or Sound, the Nām or Name, the Logos or

[6] Johnson, *Path of the Masters,* p. 334.

Word that emanates from the Ultimate and is not only identical in essence with the Supreme Spirit but is the Supreme Spirit Itself. It is the Sat Nām, the True Name, whereby the Supreme is fully manifest in the worlds of being. From the "creative center of the universe of universes" it flows out to all areas of existence in a continuous circle that takes it to the furthest level of being and returns it, in ceaseless flow, to its Source. All life and motion are caught within the outward flow, and all human souls potentially are capable of being drawn up in the returning flow and led back to the Source of the current, which, however, remains identical with the current, no matter where it may be flowing. It is to the returning wave that the Rādhā Soāmī Master points, for it is the knowledge of this current and the means of attachment to it that are his greatest gifts to seeking mankind.

It is by means of the Audible Life Stream that the Supreme Being infuses life or soul stuff into the material dimensions. Most importantly from the perspective of the souls of men, the Life Stream is *Audible,* it can be heard! The individual (manmukh) who depends upon himself will never discover its existence; the person (gurumukh) who comes into contact with a living Master will, under his loving guidance, "hear the Word" in all its beautiful forms and be carried by its current back to the Source of his being, the Source that is his True Soul.

It is the contention of the Rādhā Soāmī that all Masters throughout time have taught that the only means of salvation, or release, or self or soul-realization, is by means of the Audible Life Stream, the Shabd. And, as we have repeatedly noted, the way to attain the secret knowledge of this single final means of arriving at Truth, of being at one with Truth, of "knowing" that one is in essence already and eternally the Truth, is by placing one's whole being in all of its dimensions completely under the guidance of a living embodiment of the realized Truth, a living Master. When this is done and the Life Stream has become Audible at the core of the human self— the soul—then one has become a jīvan-mukta, a liberated free soul here and now. The Sat Guru, the Master, has directed his student and devotee to the Audible Life Stream (Shabd Dhun), the melodious word or sound that brings intuitive knowledge of one's own true nature as the eternally free Supreme Truth.

IV

We began this chapter by emphasizing the role of the "holy" person in traditional Hinduism and in present-day popular cult and piety in India. The Rādhā Soāmī Satsaṅg with its Masters is a contemporary example of that tradition and its emphasis upon the "God-man" who possesses the secret of all existence. The basic understanding of the nature of man's condition, his constituent parts, and his ultimate destiny are close duplicates of the fundamental themes associated with the Great Tradition of Hindu philosophy-theology. The authority of this tradition is appealed to by the sect as an earlier but frequently misunderstood manifestation of the same truth being taught today in a more complete form. The same traditional themes are joined with other fundamentals of historic Hindu religion, for example, popular Vaiṣṇava bhakti and the conviction that the secret is not now a hidden thing, but is made available to man through the loving grace of the Supreme One.

The means to this grace is a fusion of the ṛṣi, the ācārya, and the guru of traditional Hinduism with the guru of Sikhism and the pīr of Muslim mysticism. And, like the Logos of Christianity, the Oṃ of Hinduism, and the Sat Nām or True Name of Sikhism, the Rādhā Soāmī Shabd contains the Supreme Truth or Word made manifest among men.

Despite the sectarian variations and emphases and the divergence from many aspects of cultic and personal piety in traditional orthodox Hinduism, the Rādhā Soāmī Satsaṅg and other sects are manifestations of the Hindu-Indian religious spirit and atmosphere and are significant elements in the mainstream of contemporary Hinduism. To predict what this or any one sect will become in the future would be foolhardy; to ignore it or its counterparts would be equally irrational if one seeks to understand Hinduism in the last half of the twentieth century.

CHAPTER FIVE

HINDU RELIGION
AND CULTURE IN
INDIAN POLITICS

Previous aspects of our consideration of contemporary Hinduism frequently have indicated a close association between Hindu religion and the totality of Indian life. Such a relationship exists for any religion holding a predominate place in a society. It is preeminently true of traditional and modern India.

We in the West are generally aware of the major political changes within the Indian subcontinent since the Second World War. Briefly stated, after some decades of agitation, in 1947 the Indian peoples gained independence within the British Commonwealth and established a secular democratic state. In this process, a sizable portion of what generally had been considered an integral part of India was separated off into a nonsecular Muslim state—Pakistan. Since that partition, the existence of a Muslim state within what many Hindus consider to be the Indian homeland and the meaning of modern Indian's secularity have been among the primary factors in the Indian political mind. The issue of political sovereignty over the Jummu-Kashmir area, as important as it is in itself, has been almost more important as a constant, irritating reminder of the partition and the religious communalism at its base.

It is within this general context and amid the many varied issues peculiar to Indian national life that Hindu religion and culture are expressing themselves politically. There are few, if any, issues that do not arouse a "Hindu" response. The fact that to many Indians and non-Indians there appears to be no specifically *religious* factor involved in a particular problem does not remove the presence and pressure of a specifically Hindu religious attitude toward it and clamor about it. Despite India's claim to being a secular state, religion's involvement in politics is a central aspect of Indian national life, and it appears to some observers to be an increasing rather than a diminishing factor at both the local and the national level.

The role of religion in the nineteenth-century development of Indian cultural and political consciousness is obvious. Studies of that period and of the freedom struggle preceding independence are forced to note the religious involvement and concern of the Indian leaders "beginning with Ram Mohan Roy on through Mahatma Gandhi to Vinoba Bhave in our day." This religious-political relationship is so evident that, in the words of Paul Devanandan, "the entire nationalist compaign [was] raised to the plane of a religious crusade inspired by newfound faith in the ancestral religion." [1] While we might expect that with the diminution of the zeal accompanying the drive for independence the specifically religious fervor would disappear, we misread the situation if we assume that religion and politics go the separate ways some people mistakenly expect of them in a secular state. As Professor K. P. Karunakaran of the Indian School of International Studies has noted, "No one who knows anything about the political developments of modern India can minimise the importance of the study of the interrelation between religion and politics in the country." [2]

[1] Paul Devanandan, "Renascent Religions and Religion," in E. J. Jurji, ed., *The Ecumenical Era in Church and Society* (New York, 1959), p. 150 f.
[2] K. P. Karunakaran, *Religion and Political Awakening in India* (Meerut, 1965), p. 1.

In recent years a number of studies have been published concerning this interrelationship between traditional religions and cultures and the new national political entities emerging within their areas.[3] In many instances discussion has centered upon the degree to which the classical themes of the so-called great tradition are amenable to the inherent demands of a modern nation-state. Do the basic metaphysical presuppositions which structure the religious-cultural mind of the citizens support the new social-political structure? Are they in fundamental opposition to it? Or are they neutral in a fashion whereby the religion and its cultural attachments are at most a passive, perhaps unconscious partner in the newly conceived national political life?

Fortunately, these important theoretical considerations have also increasingly been accompanied by detailed studies of the actual behavior of religious groups and geographic, economic, and other sections of the citizens involved. And while it is dangerous to generalize in this matter, many are becoming aware that traditional religious attachments, and social identifications and adherence, do not necessarily guarantee political decisions commensurate with the tradition as outsiders have conceived it. This may well be another instance of the failure of the student of religion and culture to note the manner in which major religious traditions have achieved the stature to merit being classified as "major" religions. They possess a great ability to adapt, and it is as a result of this that they have become major factors in the individual lives and the collective societies of their areas over long periods of history.

In discerning discussions of "The Political Implications of Asian Religions" and "Emerging Patterns of Religions and Politics" in South Asia, Professor Donald E. Smith attempts to discover within the religions themselves criteria to guide their attitudes and actions

[3] For example, among others: Robert N. Bellah, ed., *Religion and Progress in Modern Asia* (New York, 1965); Karunakaran, *Religion and Political Awakening;* B. R. Purohit, *Hindu Revivalism and Indian Nationalism* (Sagar, 1965); Jerrold Schecter, *The New Face of Buddha: The fusion of religion and politics in contemporary Buddhism* (New York, 1967); Donald E. Smith, *India as a Secular State* (Princeton, 1964); Donald E. Smith, ed., *South Asian Politics and Religion* (Princeton, 1966).

in the political arena.[4] For example, he notes the "theory of History" of a religion, its "attitude toward other religions," its "capacity for ecclesiastical organization," the distribution of "political and religious functions" traditionally conceived by the religion, and its "tendency to regulate society." [5] These matters, he suggests, will reveal the religion's basic attitudes toward the importance of political action, the degree of its tolerance of diversity within the nation-state, its capacity to influence political decision-making and action, its inherited conception of its role in political leadership, and its concern with the structures of society.

Following this attempt at classifying traditional understandings of the relationship between some of the major philosophical-theological themes and the social attitudes of the religion, Professor Smith goes on to suggest emerging patterns of the participation or nonparticipation of the major religions in the present political situation of South Asia. In regard to India and Hinduism he discerns the following emerging patterns: the strong role played by religious-communal groups in political party allegiance; the absence of a governmental relationship with religious leadership, due primarily to the nonexistence of formal religious structures; the part played by government in the reform of Hindu cultic life and the supervision of temples; the support of idealism in governmental policy resulting from Hindu metaphysical principles; the presence in Indian politics of political parties revolting against the Hindu religion or certain aspects of it; and the intrusion of law as a result of governmental policy into spheres traditionally under the dominance of religion.[6]

The foregoing implications and patterns are helpful in considering the relationship between Hindu religion and culture on the one hand and the political life of the present secular state of India on the other. However, as Smith himself is aware, we cannot confine ourselves to a consideration of the classical religious attitudes alone, nor can we safely assume that previous understandings of and com-

---

[4] Smith, ed., *South Asian Politics and Religion*, pp. 3–48.
[5] *Ibid.;* see especially chart, p. 19.   [6] *Ibid.;* see especially chart, pp. 46–47.

mitments to the traditional social structure have remained or will remain unchanged. Slow to react as traditional religions may appear to be, they do change. Their fundamental themes are not as rigid and unbending as they often seem, and their ability to adapt socially while maintaining their inherent integrity is not as circumscribed as we sometimes assume. In this chapter we shall attempt to describe one instance today wherein Hindu religion and the culture assumed to be integral to it are active participants in Indian political life.

I

As we suggested earlier, Hindu religious concerns and groups were not isolated from nineteenth-century political movements in India. The role of the Ārya Samāj in North Indian politics at the end of the century and later is a case in point. Norman G. Barrier maintains that during the period 1894–1908 "the Samaj was probably the most important factor in determining the character and direction of the Punjab Congress. Association with the Arya Samaj gave educated Hindus a political orientation and an impetus to carry on political work." [7] A "religious" movement concerned with the revival and reform of Hinduism, having its basic attitudes shaped by what was held to be a "purified" understanding of the Vedas and of traditional Hinduism, served as a primary motivation for participation in political activity. A further example is found in Swāmī Vivekānanda's conception of Hindu loyalty to the "motherland" and its influence on political activity in Bengal and elsewhere. Throughout the whole period of Hindu reform and revival, both the early and the later political movements were the recipients of some of the idealism, grounding, and fervor of the religious ferment of the same period.

An outstanding example of this combination of firm religious commitment and political action is to be seen in the life and teach-

[7] Norman G. Barrier, "The Arya Samaj and Congress Politics in the Punjab, 1894–1908," *The Journal of Asian Studies* XXVI, No. 3 (May 1967), 363. See references to later Ārya Samāj activities and influence in a typical North Indian village in Oscar Lewis, *Village Life in Northern India* (New York, 1965), *passim*.

ings of Bāl Gangādhar Tilak (1856–1920).[8] Frequently referred
to as "the father of Indian Nationalism," Tilak was a Mahārāṣṭrian
Brāhman whose Hindu orthodoxy and Sanskrit learning gave him
an authoritative religious voice, while his dedication to "Swarāj," or
political independence, at great personal sacrifice gave him a heroic
status of great appeal to his countrymen.

A considerable amount of the influential impact of the ancient
religious text, the *Bhagavadgītā,* upon Indian-Hindu political leaders and educated youth in the twentieth century is the result of
Tilak's monumental *Gītā Rahasya,* the secret (upaniṣad) of the
Gītā.[9] Tilak's interpretation of the *Gītā* laid the necessary religious
base for an Indian-Hindu political and social activism. Rejecting
the contention that Hinduism is *primarily* a way of life oriented to
withdrawal from worldly concerns (an erroneous belief still all too
prevalent in the West), Tilak placed his emphasis upon "karma
yoga," the discipline of action, that along with two other yogas—
"jñāna" or knowledge, and "bhakti" or devotion—is to be found
in the *Gītā.* True, the way of mystic intuitive knowledge and the
way of adoration and devotion to the Divine are considered superior in the teachings of the *Gītā,* but they are for those individuals
who have progressed far along the spiritual path. The discipline of
action, he maintained, was the message of the incarnate god (avatāra) Kṛṣṇa for the ordinary man, the overwhelming majority of
the Indian people who are daily confronted with concrete problems.

For Tilak and a growing number of Hindus since he wrote the
Gītā Rahasya, certain qualities emphasized by the *Gītā* are essential as a base for worldly action. In sum, the individual must act
with "single-minded purposefulness" while at the same time lack-
ing any personal desire or attachment to the result of the act. And

[8] For the life and thought of Tilak see: D. V. Athalye, *The Life of Lokmanya Tilak* (Poona, 1921); D. P. Karmarkar, *Bal Gangadhar Tilak* (Bombay, 1956); G. P. Pradhan and A. K. Bhagwat, *Lokmanya Tilak* (Bombay, 1958); D. V. Tah-mankar, *Lokmanya Tilak* (London, 1956); B. G. Tilak, *His Writings and Speeches* (Madras, 1918); *Speeches* (Madras, 1918).
[9] B. S. Sukthankar, trans., *The Gītā-rahasya (of Bal Ganga Tilak)* (Bombay, 1935).

it is of supreme importance that the act be aimed toward the welfare of the world. The welfare, or betterment, of all (loksaṁgraha) is the only proper reason for action. In fact, it is the welfare of all that demands that one act.

Starting from this *religious* base, supported by his interpretation of the sacred and popular *Bhagavadgītā*, Tilak insisted that only in the ancient values of Hinduism could India find the resources necessary for swarāj. Independence must have Indian, and therefore Hindu, roots or it would not be true self-rule. Without the indigenous and proper underpinnings self-rule could not be; at best, such a rule would not be a rule by the "self" of India but one based on Western ideals and traditions. If this were to happen, India would no longer exist.

Firmly convinced, therefore, that native Indian political and social policy must be Hindu and not Western in its orientation, he opposed social reforms resulting from foreign ways of life. When India had achieved its true political and social independence then, and only then, would a Hindu government exist that represented the true will of the Indian people. This would be a "moral government" capable of creating whatever moral climate was necessary for the Motherland and its peoples under Sanātana Dharma—the eternal religion which is India's glorious heritage.

Seeking to mobilize pride in Hinduism and dedicated action toward independence, Tilak organized the celebration of two religious-political festivals that, particularly in his home area of Mahārāṣṭra, served as rallying points for political action based upon a *Hindu* awareness. One festival, ten days dedicated to the elephant-headed god Gaṇeśa (Gaṇapati), furthered Tilak's purposes in giving to its participants an awareness of their "Hinduness" in contradistinction to the foreign influences that were apparently overwhelming India politically and religiously. The second festival honors the seventeenth-century Marāthā warrior Śivājī, who in his successful struggles against the Muslim Mughal Empire proved that Hinduism could produce heroic leaders able to stand up to foreign invaders and thwart their seeming invincibility.

Tilak's rationale for the Gaṇeśa festival was an early expression of a sentiment that has continued to lie at the base of Hindu religious-political philosophy.

Such festivals are an important means of bringing about national unity. If people come together with the object of public worship their minds are moulded in a particular way and the sense of brotherhood for all fellow-worshippers is developed. Once then the mind and the heart reach a particular state of culture *it is possible to use them for other purposes as well.* How can a person be proud of his country who does not feel proud of his religion? That is how religion and nationality are interconnected.[10]

One organization that has continued to perpetuate the religious and political ideals and the fervor of the Ārya Samāj, and of leaders such as Tilak, is the Hindu Mahāsabhā. One of its early spokesmen, V. D. Savarkar (1883–1966), a youthful protégé of Tilak, played a leading role in expressing the thought still at the foundation of the prominent examples of Hinduism in politics in India. His most widely known book, *Hindutva,* lays the foundation for many present-day expositions of Hindu religious-cultural ideals in the political realm.[11] The word "Hindutva" (literally "Hinduness") was meant to convey and to include all aspects of Hindu belief and life. "Let Hinduism concern itself with the salvation of life after death, the concept of God, and the Universe. Let individuals be free to form opinions about the trio. . . . But so far as the materialistic and secular aspect is concerned, the Hindus are a nation bound by a common culture, a common history, a common language, a common country, and a common religion." [12] Savarkar, thus, meant to include more than those matters that scholars might agree pertain specifically to religion. Within "Hindutva" were included the classical philosophy-theology, the broad amorphous folk religion, *and*

[10] N. C. Keḷkar, ed., *Lokamānya Ṭiḷakāñce Kesarītīl Lekh,* Bhāg I (Poona, 1922), p. 487. Quoted in Purohit, *Hindu Revivalism,* p. 116. Italics added.
[11] V. D. Savarkar, *Hindutva* (Poona, 1949). For a biography of Savarkar see Dhananjay Keer, *Savarkar and His Times* (Bombay, 1950). This was republished in 1966 under the title *Veer Savarkar.*
[12] Savarkar, *Hindutva,* pp. 3–4. Quoted in Purohit, *Hindu Revivalism,* p. 137.

the totality of the Indian cultural and social inheritance. A participant in this inheritance is not necessarily limited to a specific religious belief or creed; he is, however, bound by a religious ethos and a cultural tradition that ties him to a fatherland, the *Bhārat-bhūmi* or "Land of India," that is both his "Fatherland and his Holyland." It is this inheritance by birth that makes him a Hindu, and he is one despite the "minor" differences separating the sects and the so-called different religions such as Buddhism, Jainism, and Sikhism. Everyone within this broad inheritance is an integral member of the "Hindu Sangathan," the Hindu organization or community.

Upon this basis, Savarkar argued, the "Hindu Rāshtra," the Hindu nation, rests both as an ancient entity and as a modern nation-state. The Hindu nation is not the present result of previous nation-forming acts of war and treaty arrangements, and it cannot be properly understood in the twentieth century if it is thought of only as a legal corporate entity created by acts of foreign governments or indigenous legislative bodies. The very basis upon which these latter agencies may act with any propriety is the Hindutva that gives the "Indian-Hindu people-religion-culture-society" its *raison d'être*.

The writings and teachings of Savarkar, associated as they are with the Hindu Mahāsabhā, however, have had their greatest influence in the field of practical party politics through the activity of an organization separate from the Mahāsabhā. This group, the Rāshtrīya Swayamsevak Sangh, or "National Volunteer Organization," interestingly enough is not a formal political party and until recently has vigorously denied interest in direct political action.[13] Generally known by its initials, the RSS came into existence in 1925 through the efforts of Dr. Keshav Baliram Hedgewar (1889–1940) of Nagpur. Educated to practice medicine, Hedgewar entered the independence struggle at an early date and soon became

---

[13] The most detailed and scholarly non-Indian study of the organization is J. A. Curran, Jr., *Militant Hinduism in Indian Politics—A Study of the R.S.S.* (New York, 1951).

convinced that a fundamental problem was the lack of proper training and organization among the Hindu people. They did not have a
sustaining consciousness of self that would equip them with the determination and resources necessary to defend themselves. They
needed a philosophy of action founded upon the historic society and
cultural community that had produced them but of which they were
only dimly aware.

Hedgewar therefore set out to create a group of highly disciplined
and indoctrinated young men constituting a militant, dedicated
core for the support and propagation of a "Hindu" consciousness among the Indian people. Little is known about the organization's early years under his leadership. Obviously, he did succeed
in creating a well-disciplined group, and on his death in 1940 the
leadership was inherited by the present head, Madhav Sadashiv
Golwalkar, who is known by his affectionate followers as "Śrī Gurujī." Since that time, the size, program, and influence of the RSS
have increased until today it has become the most important vehicle for the contemporary expression of Hindutva as conceived
by Savarkar.

Though frequently in disagreement with specific policies of the
Congress Party, and avoiding any direct political party alignment,
the RSS supported the struggle for independence. Individual members of the group were much more at home ideologically with the
Hindu Mahāsabhā than with the party of Gāndhī and Nehru, and
undoubtedly gave the former more direct political support.[14] With
the coming of freedom, accompanied as it was by the partition and
the resulting holocaust of mass migration and refugee resettlement,
the RSS quickly became identified with extreme Hindu nationalist
sentiment. It opposed both the partition and the Indian political
leadership that had accepted it. And, although it was later cleared
of any direct involvement in the assassination of Mahātma Gāndhī,
it was banned by the central government in the midst of the national suspicion of right-wing Hindu groups that followed the trag-

14 Craig Baxter, "The Jana Sangh," in Smith, ed., *South Asian Politics and Religion*, p. 76.

edy. After having been banned for approximately a year and a half, the RSS agreed to a written constitution that precluded political activities by the organization, though not by individual members, and in July 1949 resumed its role as the "organiser" [15] and educator of the peoples properly subject to Hindutva.

The partition of *Bhāratmātā,* "Mother India," into two separate nation-states, and the experience of being banned by the Congress government had a profound effect upon the thinking of the RSS and its subsequent policy in regard to participation in party politics. Whereas before it had apparently been content to emphasize its cultural-religious-social educational task in the light of Hindutva and had left any direct political participation to the individual discretion of its members, now it began to change its policy in the belief that a strong, Hindu-oriented political organization would have avoided partition and its tragic aftermath, and also would have served as a protector and voice for the ideals of the RSS when it was under attack.[16] As a result, some prominent members of the RSS began to work toward the formation of a political party separate from the RSS itself, but expressing the organization's ideals in concrete political action. In time, they received the blessing of Golwalkar in their endeavor, though his early relationship with their activity has never been clear. Given the authoritarian nature of the RSS, however, it is obvious that leading members of the group could not have been so active politically without the tacit approval of the strong RSS leader.

It has been said that the birth of the resulting political party was the "coming together of a political leader in need of an organization and an organization in need of a leader for the political aspects of its program." [17] The organization was the RSS; the political leader was Dr. Shyama Prasad Mookerjee (1901–1953).

A Bengali, Mookerjee was a brilliant academician and lawyer

[15] The function of "organizing" the people of India is considered by the RSS to be its chief mission. Hence, the name of its semiofficial weekly publication is *Organiser.*
[16] Motilal A. Jhangiani, *Jana Sangh and Swatantra* (Bombay, 1967), p. 14 f.
[17] Baxter, "The Jana Sangh," p. 74.

who had been president of the Hindu Mahāsabhā and a member of the first Nehru government following independence. By 1950 he had ceased to be a member of the Mahāsabhā and had resigned from the Nehru cabinet, primarily over disagreements about Pakistan and refugee policies. He was a political leader, well known particularly throughout North India, but was without a political organization. With his Mahāsabhā background and his commitment to the conception of Hindutva, it was but natural that he would find much in common with the religious-cultural principles of the RSS, as well as with its emerging political desires. The end result was that in 1951 Mookerjee, in close collaboration with selected members of the RSS but without official RSS participation, organized a political party known as the Bhāratīya Jana Saṅgh, the Indian People's Party. Mookerjee served as its first president until 1953, when he died under mysterious circumstances while a prisoner of the Kashmiri government on the charge of entering Kashmir without a border permit.

In the years that have passed since the party's founding the Jana Saṅgh has experienced the ups and downs one would expect for a new party in a multiparty state dominated by one overwhelmingly large, established political party enjoying the prestige of identification with the nation's attainment of freedom. And while in the general election of 1967 it gained the largest popular vote of any one party other than the Congress Party, it has remained relatively small in its parliamentary membership at the central and state levels, and in the past few years has suffered from the growing strength of Indira Gandhi's New Congress Party. Nevertheless, it is now the leading political spokesman for the ideals of Hindutva as proposed by Savarkar, expressed by Hedgewar, and today brilliantly, if erratically, preached by Śrī Gurujī Golwalkar. Earlier strong denials of a close relationship between the "political" Jana Saṅgh and the "cultural" RSS are now seldom if ever heard and, though the two remain formally distinct organizationally, the ideological guidance and directional control of the political party by the cultural organization are accepted factors in Indian political life.

II

A consideration of the principles of the Bhāratīya Jana Saṅgh as a political party is more productive if primary reference is made to the thought of the Rāshtrīya Swayaṁsevak Saṅgh. In the Jana Saṅgh, one is confronted by political policies based upon an intense nationalism and understandably shaped by the political situation at any given moment; in the RSS, there is more clearly discernible an abiding conviction that there is an appropriate, in fact, divinely ordained, foundation upon which Indian political policy and action must be based if India is to become a viable vehicle for Bhāratīya Saṅskriti, "Indian culture" and Dharma Rājya, the "rule of Spirituality." [18] The cultural organization lays the basis for the political party. Elements in one are noticeably present in the other, and the two intertwine until they become indistinguishable. Political action and Hindutva—Hindu religion, culture, and history—all become one and the same thing. To quote Golwalkar:

in Hindusthan, Religion is an all absorbing entity . . . it has become eternally woven into the life of the Race, and forms, as it were its very soul. With us every action in life, individual, social, or political, is a command of religion . . . we are what our great religion has made us. Our Race-Spirit is a child of our Religion, and so with us culture is but a product of our all-comprehensive Religion, a part of its body and not distinguishable from it.[19]

The manifesto adopted by the Jana Saṅgh at the time of its founding in 1951 said in part, "there is an atmosphere of disappointment and frustration in the country. . . . The ruling Congress party in its haste to make India a carbon-copy of the West is undermining the people's faith in the national values and ideals." [20] Commenting upon this condition and the need for the Jana Saṅgh to meet it, a former president of the party wrote that the aim of the party then and more recently has been to "develop India as a po-

[18] M. S. Golwalkar, *Bunch of Thoughts* (Bangalore, 1966), p. 68.
[19] M. S. Golwalkar, *We, or Our Nationhood Defined* (Napgur, 1947), p. 27 f, quoted in Curran, *Militant Hinduism*, p. 29.
[20] Quoted in Balraj Madhok, *Why Jana Sangh?* (Bombay, 1966), p. 6 f.

litical, social and economic democracy based on Bhāratīya Saṅ-skriti . . ." [21] It is in the frequent reference to this term "Bhāra-tīya Saṅskriti" that the central principles guiding the RSS and mo-tivating it to political action through the Jana Saṅgh are revealed.

In a collection published in 1966 of portions of his many speeches to varied audiences across India over the years, Gurujī Golwalkar lays bare the extreme pride that the Indian sometimes feels about the glories of Hindu culture in the past and its unique status as a bountiful contributor to all the world's peoples now and in the im-mediate future. Maintaining that the national distinctions of peo-ples and their separate cultures cannot and should not be eradi-cated, he says that the Hindu genius of recognizing unity amidst diversity enables the Indian people to

stand for a harmonious synthesis among nations and not their oblitera-tion. . . . the mission of reorganising the Hindu people on the lines of their unique national genius . . . is not only a great process of true national regeneration of Bharat [India] but also the inevitable precondi-tion to realize the dream of world unity and human welfare. . . . it is the grand world-unifying thought of Hindus alone that can supply the abiding basis for human brotherhood, that knowledge of the Inner Spirit which will charge the human mind with the sublime urge to toil for the happiness of mankind, while opening out full and free scope for every small life-specialty on the face of the earth to grow to its full stature. This knowledge is in the safe custody of Hindus alone. It is a divine trust, we may say, given to the charge of the Hindus by Destiny.[22]

Full confidence in the superior and divine nature of Hindu phi-losophy-theology and in its knowledge of the "Inner Spirit," and a conviction that there is a divinely ordained mission to spread abroad and implement this knowledge—these lie at the heart of RSS teaching and are revealed on a limited, more national scale in Jana Saṅgh political propaganda. Granting that in the case of the RSS the teaching is for home consumption, serving to inculcate pride in things Hindu and to win adherents for the organization, we cannot ignore the fact that it reflects a belief sincerely held by many Hin-

[21] *Ibid.*, p. 7.   [22] Golwalkar, *Bunch of Thoughts*, p. 7.

dus. It is a direct reflection of some forms of Hindu Vedānta teaching and activity, such as, for example, that of the Rāmakrishna Vedānta Society, both in India and in other parts of the world. It is a contemporary expression in almost identical language of the nineteenth-century beliefs and claims of Swāmī Dayānand Saraswatī of the Ārya Samāj, as well as those of Swāmī Vivekānanda, the founder of the Rāmakrishna Mission.

For both the RSS and the Jana Saṅgh, the initial aim is to develop a heightened awareness of the Hindu heritage and an increased loyalty to it for the purposes of creating, culturally and politically, a modern Hindu nation based upon Hindutva. According to Golwalkar, when this is accomplished then the Indian nation and its Hindu people will be prepared to implement a political program that will recreate the united motherland of the glorious Hindu past, fully equipped to perform its divine mission in the world of the present. For the cultural organization the basic goal is a call to arms for the restoration of Hindutva among Hindus, and mention of world mission is made because of the pride of superiority that it arouses rather than with serious intent at cultural expansion beyond the Indian subcontinent. For the political group it is a way to gain passionate support in its immediate aim of obtaining office, as well as to prepare the Indian people for the necessary step of establishing Hindutva throughout the geographic area that is the culture's natural homeland, including the present non-secular Muslim state of Pakistan.

Strongly objecting to the criticism of some that the attempt to revive past Hindu culture is reactionary, Golwalkar says that "rejuvenation of eternal and ennobling values of life can never be reactionary. . . . By rejuvenation of our culture we mean the reliving of those eternal life-ideals that have nourished and immortalised our national life all these millennia." [23] He is convinced that the Hindu peoples have available to them in Bhāratīya Saṅskriti the keystone to national greatness that is the only hope for them in the

[23] *Ibid.*, p. 22.

modern world. "All peoples have it as their duty to search for the riches of their past and to make them meaningful for their corporate life in the present." [24]

Readily admitting that one cannot define Hindu culture, Golwalkar insists that Hindus can feel it: "our sentiments, ideals, and aspirations have a reality of their own and have a very vital role in our life even though they cannot be expressed in terms of definitions. . . ." [25] Culture manifests itself within the total society in such a manner that the sensitive person is drawn to its high values by an inner compulsion beyond mere intellect or educational training.

Hindu culture manifests itself in Indian national life first by "the urge for realisation of the Supreme Being permeating the entire universe." Man wants a living God that "will engross us in activity and invoke all the powers that reside in our being." From the earliest Hindu sages down through Rāmakrishna and Vivekānanda wise men have taught that "the Hindu People . . . is the *Virāt Purusha,* the Almighty manifesting Himself." The ancient teaching which describes the sun and moon as the eyes of the Almighty, and the stars and the skies as being created from his navel, also declares that the "Brāhmin is the head, King the hands, Vaishya the thighs and Shūdra the feet. This means that the people who have this fourfold arrangement [the varṇa structure of Hindu society], i.e, the Hindu People, is our God." [26]

Golwalkar holds that it is because of the foregoing that the true "Swayaṁsevak," the volunteer or adherent of the RSS, sees every member of Hindu society as a part of the Divine Whole. Everyone is sacred and worthy of service from others. As a result, in Bhāratīya Sanskriti, the culture best described by Hindutva, "the spirit of social service has been sublimated into worship of God." God is to be worshipped and served in the form of society, and when the Hindu is rightfully aware of the manifestation of his sacred and

---

[24] Statement made in a personal interview with the author, New Delhi, Oct. 25, 1967.
[25] Golwalkar, *Bunch of Thoughts,* p. 23.   [26] *Ibid.,* pp. 24 f.

traditional culture he is instinctively led to be a trustee of that divinely ordained culture, responsible for its firm establishment among the Indian people.[27] The divine nature of the culture gives it a mandate placing it above human considerations of personal desires and selfish motivations. "The RSS ideal of the individual's duty without personal rights or privilege is a direct product of the highest teaching of Bhāratīya Sanskriti and dominates all who come under RSS influence."[28] Also, this culture has at its center the conviction that "Truth is one, sages call it variously." This results in a respect, not tolerance or sufferance, but an acceptance of other faiths and viewpoints as being acceptable paths to attain the same Truth.[29]

Here, again, we have further manifestations of basic tenets associated with the classical formulations of Hindu philosophy-theology, tenets that are frequently at the heart of the teaching of present-day Hindu religious sects. The "eternal and ennobling values" that Golwalkar is seeking to rejuvenate among the Indian people are fundamental themes recurring throughout Hindu literature. The identity of the individual with the Ultimate as expressed in the Advaita of Śankara; the varṇa divisions of human society identified in the Ṛgveda with the body of Puruṣa and sanctioned by the ancient Laws of Manu; the call to duty and service without consideration of one's self as taught by Kṛṣṇa to Arjuna in the Bhagavadgītā— all these are part of the idealism that has been at the core of Hindu thought for millennia. Hindu revivalists and reformers for over a hundred years have sought to make them meaningful again to the Indian people, as they believe they were in the golden days of India's past. The RSS and the Jana Sangh seek to make them viable among the people and in the society of the modern nation-state of India; and they are convinced that this can be done fully only when these ideals are at the base of political policy and action, as well as being well-springs for individual personal life.

[27] Ibid., pp. 25–27.
[28] Statement of Śrī Golwalkar in a personal interview with the author, New Delhi, Oct. 25, 1967.
[29] Golwalkar, Bunch of Thoughts, p. 27.

An important aspect of RSS and Jana Saṅgh thought is best illustrated by the apparently loose use of the words "Bhāratīya" and "Hindu." It will be noticed that in the preceding paragraphs these two words and the term "Indian" have been used interchangeably and without any distinction between them. We have followed RSS and Jana Saṅgh practice deliberately here because it is essential that we be aware of the apparent confusion of the words and what they convey—a confusion that is not present in the minds of the leadership of the two groups, and which they insist is the result of the "mischievous propaganda" of the British during the nineteenth century.[30]

Discussing the origins and varied usages of the names given to the people residing in the geographic area of the subcontinent, Gurujī Golwalkar declares that all of them, with the exception of "Hindu," are misleading. Even "Bhāratīya" with its ancient origin and honored place in Indian literature leads to a misconception because it is translated into English today as "Indian." Indian, he says, "includes all the various communities like the Muslim, Christian, Parsi etc., residing in this land . . . when we want to denote our particular society. . . . 'Hindu' *alone* connotes correctly and completely the meaning that we want to convey." [31] It should be noted that the specific communities he names and does not wish to include—the Muslim, Christian, Parsi—are all of non-Indian origin. The Jain, Buddhist, and Sikh communities, all having their origin in India, are not singled out for distinction from "Hindu" as understood within the context of Hindutva.

Denying that the name "Hindu" is recent in origin, or that it was first used by foreigners, he claims that especially for the last thousand years the leaders and the great of India have "taken the name 'Hindu' to denote our people and our *dharma*. . . . The name 'Hindu' . . . has thus become a word that at once reflects the unity, the sublimity, and the specialty of our people." [32] His use here of the word "Dharma" is revealing. We have briefly dis-

<hr>

[30] *Ibid.*, p. 97.   [31] *Ibid.*, p. 98. Italics added.   [32] *Ibid.*, p. 98 f.

cussed its significance in a previous context.[33] We need here only to remind ourselves that whether broadly defined as "the Hindu way of life," "the moral law," "propriety," "duty," or whatever, Hindu writers in almost all instances refer to the "scriptural and religious sanction" that supports it. As Joan Bondurant and Margaret Fisher have stated, *"dharma* is religion in the broadest sense." [34] The RSS leader by his strong preference for the word "Hindu" clearly reveals the spiritual, supramundane—religious—foundation that is believed to support "the unity, the sublimity, and the specialty" of the Hindu-Indian people.

This conviction of the divine sanction and destiny of the Hindu people and their social entity, the present Indian nation-state, is manifested in the many instances where Gurujī Golwalkar expresses a firm faith that the nation can surmount apparently insuperable odds if it is faithful to the Dharma that is its sacred inheritance. To cite but one example, the military confrontations with Pakistan and China in recent years:

Let us not be unnecessarily alarmed about the evil combination of China and Pakistan. We can most certainly bring to knees both the aggressors. . . . Indeed it would have been highly desirable if China had followed up its ultimatum and invaded our country. . . . The world would then have witnessed the supreme heights of our Bharatiya heroism, for what fun is there in merely fighting a petty power like Pakistan? [35]

And in another context, he quotes Sister Niveditā, the disciple of Swāmī Vivekānanda: "If only Hindus collectively pray daily for ten minutes in the morning and in the evening, they will become an invincible society." [36] Examples of similar statements could be given almost endlessly.

[33] *Supra,* p. 65 f.
[34] Joan Bondurant and Margaret Fisher, "The Concept of Change in Hindu, Socialist, and Neo-Gandhian Thought," in Smith, ed., *South Asian Politics and Religion,* p. 242.
[35] Golwalkar, *Bunch of Thoughts,* p. 310 f.
[36] *Ibid.,* p. 368.

Turning briefly to the statements of the concrete political expression of the cultural ideals of the RSS, the announced program and policies of the Bhāratīya Jana Saṅgh reveal a pragmatic political realism that is, nevertheless, informed by the more passionate, frequently demagogic, utterances of the RSS and its charismatic leader. It must be remembered that the core working leadership of the Jana Saṅgh, though not always its more public political figures, came directly from the RSS and has remained openly identified with their discipline and intense comradely dedication to the leadership of their Gurujī.[37] And despite Golwalkar's denials that the RSS dominates the Jana Saṅgh,[38] the present open relationship of the two in terms of ideals, policies, support of specific programs, and actual leadership makes the denial appear to be a mere façade to meet the limitation upon the organization's participation in direct political activity imposed by the Congress-dominated government in 1949.

An inclusive and general public statement of party principles and policies entitled *Why Jana Sangh?* was written shortly before the 1967 general elections by the then president of the Jana Saṅgh and a member of the Lokh Sabhā, Professor Balraj Madhok.[39] In the realm of foreign policy the existence of Pakistan and the threat from China were the two most immediate and primary considera-

[37] The fifteen-year tenure of the late Deendayal Upadhyaha as general secretary of the Jana Saṅgh and his election as president of the party in December 1967 present an outstanding instance of this relationship. He came directly into Jana Saṅgh work from an important role in the RSS. His mysterious death in February 1968 has made him a martyr in the eyes of both the RSS and the Jana Saṅgh. See also Jhangiani, *Jana Sangh and Swatantra*, pp. 188 ff.

[38] Made publicly and frequently, and personally to the author in October 1967 by the statement, "we could have if we had wanted to." This was said in an interview at the home of the Mayor of New Delhi, a Jana Saṅgh party member, and in the presence of the then general secretary of the party, Deendayal Upadhyaha, two or three Jana Saṅgh members of the Lokh Sabhā (parliament), a small group of party leaders, and the brilliant editor of the semiofficial RSS (and Jana Saṅgh?) weekly paper, the *Organiser*, K. R. Malkani.

[39] Madhok, *Why Jana Sangh?* This was one of a series of pamphlets each of which was written by a spokesman for a different Indian political party, and issued shortly before the general election. See also Jhangiani, *Jana Sangh and Swatantra*, pp. 44–105.

tions. Concerning Pakistan Madhok said, "Pakistan . . . is and will continue to be India's born enemy, so long as it exists in its present form," and he insisted that both the USA and the USSR "have their own interests in India" and wanted "to preserve and strengthen Pakistan as a counter balance to India." Both of them, he charged, had demanded and gotten a high price from India for the support they had given it, while demanding little or nothing from Pakistan. The "U.S.S.R. forced Tashkent Declaration on us and U.S.A. forced devaluation of Indian rupee on us." The Jana Saṅgh maintained that similar demands would be made by the great powers, and India would be helpless before those demands until she gave priority to the development of military resources sufficient for her to protect herself from the threats of Pakistan and China, or any other nation. And, basically, this could only be done by following policies that would develop military self-reliance, create a base for flexible and reciprocal relationships with other countries in place of a continuing tendency to follow blindly the old Nehru policy of nonalignment, and, above all, in every way free India from dependence upon the USSR and the USA.[40]

The economic policy put forth by the Jana Saṅgh is oriented toward free enterprise rather than toward the qualified state socialism advocated by the old Congress Party or the more widely practiced state socialism prescribed by Mrs. Gandhi's New Congress. The Jana Saṅgh accuses the government of creating state monopolies resulting in a diminishing private sector of economic activity, inefficiency, curbing of competition, and especially a depreciation of the individual and his freedom. In its place the Jana Saṅgh would emphasize the development of a free economy with state activity severely limited to those areas of economic endeavor where private capital is insufficient. The party's main contention is that the state should remove itself from its present monopolistic position in many areas of economic activity. Its primary function should be the creation of a political atmosphere conducive to free, competitive economic enterprise. The state's primary responsibility

40 Madhok, *Why Jana Sangh?* pp. 8–13.

beyond the creation of such an atmosphere is the prevention of monopolistic control by any one element, public or private. In many ways the economic program of the Jana Saṅgh is Western in regard to industry, and modern in its emphasis on the creation of an industrial complex that could give India a self-sufficient economic viability. And it is Indian or nationalistic in its belief that foreign companies, for example, those in the oil industry, should be "Indianized." This means that they should become privately controlled Indian enterprises, not socialistic, government-controlled industries.[41]

At the level of village and agricultural life, the party has accused the government of ignoring the long-range importance and immediate need for investment in agriculture because of its overriding concern with state industrialism. Here the party's emphasis is on traditional small-area farming made more productive by increased irrigation, better fertilization, and government assurance of proper prices for food products. Generally speaking, with a few exceptions, it maintains that Western-style mechanization of agriculture is unrealistic for India. Its firm opposition to cow slaughter as running counter to the whole Hindu religious-cultural-psychological tradition, a central tenet of RSS teaching, is also given an economic base; for example, Madhok states that "it is the better, well-fed cows and bulls, that are being butchered and not the useless and uneconomic cattle. That makes the need for total ban on slaughter of cows and bulls, a pressing economic necessity." [42]

It is in the realm of social policy that the "Hindu" nature of the Jana Saṅgh is most evident. Attacking Western and primarily the English form of education followed in India, it demands the Indianization of the educational system:

"Absence of moral and national content in the education curricula, is a basic flaw in the present system of education, which was imposed on us by the British to create clerks and a class of mental slaves. . . . The continued imposition of English on the young boys has made the situation worse. Whatever little moral content in educational curricula had

41 *Ibid.,* p. 21.   42 *Ibid.,* p. 19.

been before freedom, has since been [voided] in the name of secularism and Indian nationalism has been reduced to idolatrous praise of Pandit Nehru and Maulana Azad, the two architects of our educational system since freedom. One was more Arab and the other was more an Englishman than Indian. . . . Jana Saṅgh stands for making the education an instrument for imbibing in the new generation a strong sense of nationalism and patriotism and a burning faith in the Indian ideals and values of life.[43]

The party has also suggested the advisability of using indigenous ancient educational ways (gurūkul) with more modern methods of instruction,[44] and here as at other points makes a strong appeal to pride in the Hindu past.

The RSS and Jana Saṅgh position concerning one of the most persistent, baffling, and volatile problems for the modern Indian state, that of language, has also created a serious political problem for the party as it seeks widespread all-India support. Both organizations have been vehement in their espousal of Hindi as the national language, and have demanded that it be incorporated into the basic educational system throughout India. However, the complications of the language problem, its regional ramifications in terms of cultural traditions, loyalties, and practical difficulties of instruction, and the political liabilities that have accrued to the Jana Saṅgh in the South and elsewhere because of its identification with a North Indian language—all have combined to bring about increasingly more moderate public expression about the matter by the party. There is little doubt, however, as to where the party stands. The ingenuity that it shows on this point, its receptivity to compromise solutions such as the "three-language formula" (e.g., native language, Hindi, English; or Hindi, another Indian language, English), its willingness to work patiently for a solution over a long rather than a short time, will be a gauge of its practical political wisdom and its potential as a majority government party of a united India. There are few in South India who will agree that "Hindi in fact is already the *lingua franca* of the country," as Madhok in-

[43] *Ibid.*, p. 24 f.   [44] Jhangiani, *Jana Sangh and Swatantra*, p. 91.

sists; [45] and there are many for whom Hindi is not the native tongue who might become enthusiastic Jana Saṅgh supporters were it not for its Hindi platform. Their attraction for the Jana Saṅgh but reluctance to support it because of its Hindi position is reflected in the following comment made to the author by a young South Indian Brāhman;

I am very interested in the policies and platforms of the RSS and the Jana Saṅgh [he said]. There are many young educated like myself who emotionally agree with what they say about most things like, for example, cow protection. After all, once a year we literally worship the cow for three days. But when the RSS and the Jana Saṅgh attack English, the language in which we received our higher education and that is the means for our intellectual reflection, let alone our professional advancement and status, and, further, insist that eventually a foreign language, Hindi, must supplant our native tongue, then we must say "No!"

Despite recent Jana Saṅgh moderation in the matter, and claims to the contrary, the cultural base to which it appeals in its plea for the support of the Indian people and the RSS Hindutva ideology which informs all theory lying behind its practical policies combine to remind the non-Hindi-speaking Indian that both organizations are possible enemies of his more localized native culture.

The problem of national versus regional traditions and loyalties in regard to language is not limited, of course, to that issue alone. The RSS has insisted upon the unity of the Indian people, and the Jana Saṅgh has sought to make this a stronger political reality. For example, it has called for a constitutional revision that would strengthen the central government and put an end to the interstate rivalry arising from the present federated national structure. Politically the Jana Saṅgh gains much of its strength from its strong appeals to all-India nationalism, though at the same time this position prevents its success at the polls in many areas of India.

The appeal for unity among all peoples from whatever linguistic, regional, caste, and local cultural backgrounds reveals itself through-

[45] Madhok, *Why Jana Sangh?* p. 26.

out Jana Sangh policies in the social area. When he was president
of the party, Professor Madhok stated that

The existence of different castes, communities and languages is a reality
of the Indian life, which no one can ignore. They cannot be wiped out.
The people have their loyalty to caste, religion and linguistic groups.
There is nothing wrong in it provided such loyalties are not allowed to
take the better of the overall loyalty to the country and the nation.
This can be achieved by strengthening Indian nationalism and empha-
sising the factors of unity.[46]

And the appeals that he made for that all-India unity, like those of
Golwalkar, are based on ancient Hindu texts and on the "purified"
understanding of Hindu religion, culture, and society identified with
the Hindu revivalist-reformers of the nineteenth century. Caste, religion, language, social custom, family relationships, social responsibility—all are to be understood and practiced in the spirit of
Hindutva, the new Hinduism that is also the old, true Hinduism of
the ancient forefathers of the present Hindu people.

The majority of Indians have not actively accepted the principles
of the RSS, and they have not supported the policies of the Jana
Sangh. Indeed, some object when a non-Indian reveals an interest
in these two groups because he believes them to be important within
modern India, to both its religion and its politics. However, to ignore them would contribute to a continuation of much of the Western misunderstanding of modern trends in both India and Hinduism.

[46] *Ibid.*, p. 27.

CHAPTER SIX

THE HINDU PROMISE
AND ITS
DILEMMA

In the preceding chapters we have attempted to consider some essential aspects of Hinduism in the latter half of the twentieth century. In each instance we have sought to focus upon elements that appear to us to constitute important factors in the Hinduism of today as it is now operative among the Indian people, their society, and the culture of which it is an integral part. Obviously, our selection has been limited, and other elements could have been chosen. What we have considered can only serve as an incomplete, but we hope helpful, indication of current trends within Hinduism as it moves from its ancient antecedents into the future.

Alfred North Whitehead once wrote: "when we consider what religion is for mankind, and what science is, it is no exaggeration to say that the future course of history depends upon the decision of this generation as to the relations between them." He insisted that a careful study of history indicates that both have always been in a state of continual development.[1] As we conclude our consideration of Hinduism it would appear to be helpful to substitute the word "modernity" for "science" in Whitehead's statement. An appraisal of the contemporary religious situation in India requires a recognition that the future course of Indian history depends upon the decision of this and immediately succeeding generations as to the relations between Hinduism and modernity. This is self-evident.

And it is equally obvious that, like science, its major component, modernity by its very nature is the complete antithesis of stasis. The condition of modernity is one in which change is paramount. Professor Shils in a discussion of "Modern States" notes that it is essential that they be "dynamic," and maintains that the educated elite within new "becoming modern" states recognize that not only must they "not fear change," they "must strive to bring it about." [2] David Lerner insists that modernization includes a "disquieting positivist spirit" touching "public institutions as well as private aspirations." [3] Certainly, an essential precondition to modernity is the will to bring about changes, great or small, that it is hoped will increase the possibility of enrichment of the society, its people, and their culture.

However, it is not evident that people today also recognize that religion—Hinduism in this instance—is always in a state of continual development. We misread the history of religion if we do not clearly discern the adaptability of the long-enduring religions. Though their most devout adherents may argue that they have endured because the truth they possess is eternal and indestructible, the student of religion notes that it is those religions possessing an aptitude for accommodation that have continued over long periods of changing circumstances to have relevance to personal human life and collective human society. Vital religion possesses the necessary sensitivity to be aware of the changing needs of men's minds, men's

[1] Alfred North Whitehead, *Science and the Modern World* (New York, 1949), p. 180 f.

[2] Edward Shils, *Political Development in the New States* (The Hague, 1966), p. 7.

[3] David Lerner, *The Passing of Traditional Society* (Glencoe, 1958), quoted in M. N. Srinivas, *Social Change in Modern India* (Berkeley, 1966), p. 50.

social conditions, and men's spiritual requirements. Such religion is by the circumstance of its environment in a constant state of development and flux, though not necessarily of radical change. As a result of this relationship with its environment, religion is potentially, if not actually, relevant to men and societies that are also undergoing a similar process. The periods of stultifying lethargy in the history of any of the world's great religions should not be allowed to blind us to the process of change that makes a religion what it is today.

Hinduism and India obviously are involved today in processes peculiar to their specific society and culture, as well as being caught up in the worldwide currents of change that mark our times. There is no question that Hinduism possesses a primary trait of traditionalism under which change comes slowly and often almost imperceptibly. For the broad masses of Hindus to turn from the tradition they believe to be the result of ancient revelation (śruti) would be to digress from what is divinely ordained and, therefore, proper in all ages. This conservatism, a characteristic not limited to Hinduism, is so well recognized by students of Indian affairs that it tends to obscure any contrary traits within the religion.

True, significant change reaching beyond limited areas or groups, so that it penetrates meaningfully and noticeably throughout wider Hinduism, is not discernible without effort. Nevertheless, there are currents present and conditions conducive to rethinking and restatement in the realm of the thematic great tradition. These same factors are not without influence upon the cultic and social structures that have long accompanied the intellectual aspects of that tradition. As a result they, also, are now subject to alteration and innovation by the educated and modern members of the society. Even within the atmosphere of the village and its folk religion, the "timeless present" is not totally unaware of the "dynamic now" surrounding and challenging it. Studies of village and rural India, while they note the strong tendency of the Indian people to remain close to traditional structures, further observe that the environment and mood are such that these tradition-bound people are also confronted by changing opportunities and that, to quote one such study, they "will not reject uncritically the benefits of new cultural elements." [4]

Professor Norman Brown has suggested that a careful examination reveals a marked degree of tolerance in India in many periods of its history. Here he is not referring to the religious tolerance we hear so much about, and which may be more an indifference to rather than a tolerance of religious variety. Brown is pointing rather to "a tolerance of the new, the unusual, and the different, a capacity to reshape itself in changing conditions, a quickness of comprehension, and a willingness to seek for new solutions to new problems." [5]

As we endeavor to understand twentieth-century Hinduism and the society and culture with which it is involved, it is essential that we realize that Indian-Hindu society today is not an absolutely static traditional society confronting modernization. The situation is more correctly understood as one in which a changing traditional society is slowly being transformed into a modern society which is also continually changing. It is not a case of an immovable structure being invaded by a well-organized and clearly defined presently exterior system. Rather, it is a process of mutual interaction between two dynamic and evolving entities. When modernity is not only conceived as something having its *primary* early origins outside a social-cultural entity, but then believed to continue as a separate structure or component in contradistinction to the social-cultural system, both the modernizing process and the social-cultural complex are all too frequently misunderstood. The interiorization of modernization is not recognized, and the important indigenous aspects of the process are easily overlooked. [6] As Pro-

[4] S. C. Dube, *Indian Village* (Ithaca, 1955), p. 234.
[5] Norman Brown, "Class and Cultural Tradition in India," in Milton Singer, ed., *Traditional India: Structure and Change* (Philadelphia, 1959), p. 39.
[6] See the discussion of this problem in Wilfred Cantwell Smith, "Traditional Religions and Modern Culture," *in Proceedings of the XIth International Congress of the International Association for the History of Religions* (3 vols., Leiden, 1968), I, 55–72.

fessors Redfield and Singer noted in their study of "The Cultural Role of Cities," in the evolving of a culture's great tradition and its later heterogenetic transformation as it confronts alien influences, often neither the original cultural development nor the subsequent transformation are discontinuous.[7] As the latter—the transformation—comes into being it is often involved with a great tradition that is itself continuous in its process of becoming.

A primary problem for us, as for students of most aspects of present-day India, centers around the involved question of the relationship—perhaps identity—between the chief religion of India and the fabric that constitutes the culture of the region. Can we discuss the situation, problems, and possibilities of Hinduism the religion in isolation from the equally large context of India the modern state, the complexities of her social structure, and the peculiar genius of the culture involved with the area and its history? Obviously, we cannot. Nor in this context can we do more than briefly refer to the problem.

Modern interpretations of Indian culture have generally fallen into two broad classifications.[8] The first has identified Hindu culture with Indian culture, suggesting that the operating norm for the latter has been the great tradition of the Hindu religion and the social structures and customs that have accompanied that tradition. This we saw most clearly in the political area—for example, in the Jana Sangh's ideological platform and its attempt to direct modern Indian political activity.

The other interpretation, namely, that India's culture is a composite not to be identified with the term "Hindu," has been more realistic in recognizing that contemporary Indian culture, like all widespread and long enduring cultures, has been the product of many influences, from the early Dravidian of thirty-five or more hundred years ago down to the British and Western of the last

[7] Robert Redfield and Milton Singer, "The Cultural Role of Cities," *Economic Development and Cultural Change* (October 1954), III, 53–73.
[8] See, for example, in relation to Indian politics and religion, D. E. Smith, *India as a Secular State,* pp. 374 ff.

hundred or two hundred years. This approach recognizes the variables and imponderables that at any given time work together to constitute a culture. Indian thinkers who adhere to this position have also emphasized with pride India's powers of assimilation and its potential as a cultural model for the modern world. This view reflects something of both the position of the nineteenth-century reform movements and the social-cultural ambivalence of the liberal intellectual and political elite of the twentieth century.

However, it is questionable whether it is wise to allow present-day scholarly knowledge about the nature of the development and composition of cultures to obscure the emotional and psychological relationship between Indian culture and Hindu religion. It may be agreed that the broad culture of twentieth-century India is not exclusively Hindu. In company with many Indians, non-Indians may challenge the strongly emotional statements affirming the identity of the two by Rāshtrīya Swayaṁsevak Saṅgh and Jana Saṅgh leaders in politics, and conservative leaders in religion who take a similar position. But we do need to be careful that such an understanding on our part does not blind us to the inherent genius of India and its culture; namely, the Hindu philosophical-theological thought patterns, the social structures and habits that in one form or another accompany them, *and* the folk religion and cult central to the "Hindu" life of India's peoples. Annie Besant's extreme emotional attachment to Hinduism and to India should not cause us to discount the following statement she made: "Make no mistake. Without Hinduism India has no future. Hinduism is the soil into which India's roots are struck, and torn out of that she will inevitably wither, as a tree torn out from its place. . . . Let Hinduism go, Hinduism that was India's cradle, and in that passing would be India's grave." [9]

One further matter needs mention among the many things that would be demanded in a more detailed discussion of both modernity and culture. This is the inherently disruptive nature of cultural interaction when that interaction occurs between a dynamic

[9] Quoted without reference in R. C. Zaehner, *Hinduism*.

force and a primarily traditional one. Relatively peaceful and slow-paced interaction does not produce the disruptive tensions and frequent chaos that is so characteristic of newly emerging political states today. In a discussion of "Westernization and the Theory of Cultural Borrowing" [10] in regard to the Muslim world, Professor Gustave von Grunebaum notes that it is the fact that interaction is "imposed from outside," is in such marked degree political in nature, and is the result of "a series of emergency situations over which the would-be borrower has but limited control" that makes the cultural interaction of the past century so disruptive to non-Western areas of the world.

The Western consciousness of the power of modernity and predisposition to doubt the flexibility of traditional societies frequently led earlier Western scholars to emphasize the obvious disruption without discerning possible indigenous means for transforming it into a potential good. In the context of his consideration of Islam as it has been confronted with Westernization and modernization, von Grunebaum describes a culture as "a 'closed' system of questions and answers concerning the universe and man's behavior in it which has been accepted as authoritative by a human society." He concludes that "as the experience of the community changes, the power to formulate and answer new questions in terms of the traditional values and the decisions previously arrived at will indicate a culture's ability to continue." [11] If we are even to begin to comprehend modern trends in Hinduism and the significance of those trends for the future of India and its religion, we must seek to determine whether Hindu religion and Indian culture have the resources to rise above the inevitable disruption accompanying contemporary cultural interaction and, indeed, have the "power to formulate and answer new questions in terms of the traditional values and the decisions previously arrived at."

[10] In "Islam: Essays in the Nature and Growth of a Cultural Tradition," *The American Anthropologist*, 57, No. 2 (April 1955), Part 2, Memoir No. 81, pp. 241 ff.
[11] *Ibid.*, p. 243.

I

If we first look at the great tradition in the light of its "power to formulate and answer new questions in terms of the traditional values," it is quickly evident that in recent years the essential themes constituting that tradition have not been considered seriously threatened by their reflective adherents. In regard to these matters, resting ultimately upon a faith commitment arising largely out of environmental conditioning and ethos, modernity has not posed for such people an absolute choice between itself and the inheritance of the past. The intellectual expression of these themes has found within contemporary rational norms and procedures standards it considers appropriate for both the advocacy and justification of the themes. These fundamental presuppositions of the Hindu mind-set, while not necessarily self-evident and viable to the non-Hindu, are just that to the Indian for whom they constitute both the traditional wisdom of the past and the key to an understanding of the present.

Having a suprarational foundation, as they ultimately do, the themes are not considered to be removed from either the formulation or the solution of contemporary questions. On the contrary, the value of the tradition is held to reside not only in its antiquity but also in its modern applicability. The tradition has not lost its supramundane and, therefore, absolutist quality. Rather, this essential quality is held to be made manifest by the present relevance which its adherents claim is self-evident. Outsiders may doubt this contention; participants within the tradition are only spurred to greater efforts to defend and express it.

The foregoing, however, may be nothing but the defense that is to be expected from the adherents of a tradition. It does not establish the ability of that tradition to meet the continuingly new that is produced by the inherent nature of modernity. Only events themselves will prove or disprove the contentions of various advocates in such a situation. Nevertheless, studies of cultural and social customs and, more pertinently, of great thematic philosophical-theological traditions and their histories do give us grounds for objecting to the still-prevalent Western tendency to underestimate the power and flexibility of non-Western traditions in their confrontation with modernity.

Professor Shils notes that "traditions often possess sufficient ambiguity and hence flexibility to allow innovations to enter without severely disruptive consequence." Recognizing that tradition does have an inherent quality that leads to a continual buttressing of itself, he is also convinced by his studies that tradition is not a "rigorously unitary whole" uniformly objecting to and impeding innovations.[12] Professor Singer, similarly, concludes in relation to the orthodox Vedānta position that "there is a kind of built-in flexibility . . . which permits an easy incorporation of a wide variety of changes." As a result, those individuals who are charged with decision-making within the tradition and its structure are able within certain limitations to change tradition, "so long as they regard the change as primarily preservative of the tradition's essentials." [13]

For all too long the Western student of non-Western cultures and societies, belonging as he does to a "modern" culture and its attendant society, has been convinced that tradition within non-modern areas must inevitably disappear before the onslaughts of modernity. As Lloyd and Susanne Rudolph in their brilliant study of political development in India clearly demonstrate,

the assumption that modernity and tradition are radically contradictory rests on a misdiagnosis of tradition as it is found in traditional societies, a misunderstanding of modernity as it is found in modern societies, and a misapprehension of the relationship between them. . . . The misunderstanding of modern society that excludes its traditional features is paralleled by a misdiagnosis of traditional society that underestimates its modern potentialities.[14]

---

12 Shils, *Political Development in the New States*, p. 32.
13 Milton Singer, "The Great Tradition in a Metropolitan Center: Madras," in *Traditional India: Structure and Change*, p. 179 f.
14 Lloyd I. and Susanne Hoeber Rudolph, *The Modernity of Tradition: Political Development in India* (Chicago, 1967), pp. 3–5.

However, these and similar conclusions by scholars whose studies are highly valued point primarily in the direction of future possibilities for the great tradition of Hinduism. They do not remove the fundamental dilemma presently confronting Hindu religion and India. This dilemma arises from the close identification of the thematic tradition with the long-existent social structure, custom morality, and religious cult patterns. These, rather than the traditional philosophical-theological themes, are now confronted by modernity in a manner threateningly disruptive of Indian life and Hindu tradition. If we consider carefully the reform and revival movements we observed briefly in chapter II, we note immediately that the reformers and revivalists did not turn away from the great themes, but in fact emphasized them as the core fundamentals of Hindu truth and the foundation of Indian social-cultural values. So, also, today the Indian voices raised in question of or opposition to the great thematic presuppositions are almost negligible.

What is being questioned as a result of the process of modernity is the body of social and custom structures that have been identified traditionally with the *proper* Hindu life. These, while giving identity to people, are slowly coming to be recognized as contributing to the separation of those same people. The custom morality that has given value to individual and communal acts is now occasionally charged with failing to question the worth of those acts in the light of the best interests of the individual and society. The cultic patterns that have supported the Hindu spiritual pilgrimage are now sometimes indicted as substitutes for the goals being sought rather than aids to their attainment.

This is not a dilemma peculiar to Hindu religion nor to the developing Indian state. It is in not unfamiliar terms the statement of the problem of similar well-established societies and cultures, no matter what their level, as they confront modernity from the perspective of their own traditions in like areas of life. The fact that these problems are not limited to Hinduism and to India does not ease the dilemma, nor remove our concern, but it does indicate something of the nature of the worldwide confrontation between modernity and tradition, and Hindu India's similarity with other religious-cultural areas.

In specific instances within the fabric of Hindu-Indian life, changes obviously are taking place, sometimes almost imperceptibly, occasionally more noticeably. Technological changes that accompany modernity do result, for example, in "abbreviation" of Hindu cultic observance to the point where the casual observer may hastily conclude that the cult will disappear; yet the same technology is furnishing the means for a wider communication of the values that the cult seeks to disseminate and preserve. Education at least partly in tune with modernity is furnishing the needed information with which searching questions are being formulated in regard to long-established customs and morality.

The dilemma, however, is clearly evident. Are the elements so closely identified with traditional Hindu religion and ways of life, especially at the folk level, capacle of continued meaning and force in the midst of modernity? Caste cohesiveness and exclusiveness; the communal or joint family with its responsibility for carrying the tradition over from one generation to the next; the Epic and Purāṇic literature and their derivative arts serving as means for the continuing inculcation of the tradition among the masses; the all-Indian and local cults reinforcing the folk beliefs and habits of centuries—do these have the power to comprehend the new conditions and accompanying questions in terms of traditional values and previous decisions? Or are they doomed to give way before already existent and yet-to-be-created structures? And if they do succumb, does this mean that Hinduism as now understood and as a discernible, continuing historical entity will cease to be?

II

Each of the traditional elements of Hindu-Indian life that we have just referred to has received a large amount of attention from professional students of Indian society. In each instance, authorities are forced by the ambiguity of the facts to qualify their conclusions. This, of course, is inevitable, given the breadth and diversity of Indian social structures and conditions of life. Frequently some less careful studies have been led to false conclusions by the insistence of Westernized or expatriate Indians that in all these matters India is rapidly moving away from the habits of the past.

Caste is a good case in point. It is a common occurrence to meet Indians in the West, and Indian apologists in India, who confidently affirm that caste is rapidly disappearing, or who insist that caste is now being understood in a new light without the disabilities and social limitations of the past. It is true that in some instances the restrictions and debilitating social separations of the past are less marked, as we noted in our study of Indian university students. Nevertheless, Indian and non-Indian scholars are almost unanimous in concluding that caste remains central both at the personal level and in the larger social structure. This is not to suggest that caste as it actually is, or as ideally formulated by some, is an unmitigated evil. But we do insist that it is not inevitably succumbing before contemporary events. The leading Indian sociologist of today, Professor M. N. Srinivas, maintains that "the power and activity of caste has increased in proportion as political power passed increasingly to the people from the [former] rulers." [15] And he insists that "caste is so tacitly and so completely accepted by all, including those who are most vocal in condemming it, that it is everywhere the unit of social action." [16] C. D. Deshmukh, one of the most respected leaders in Indian intellectual life and a former cabinet minister, is forced to say: "it cannot be said that even in urban areas caste is on the way out, and in rural areas it is strongly entrenched. Its misuse for personal gain by political leaders has given a new lease of life to caste notwithstanding professions to the contrary." [17] Oscar Lewis in his study of village life notes that the economic and social changes that are occurring "will

[15] M. N. Srinivas, *Caste in Modern India and Other Essays* (Bombay, 1962), p. 23.
[16] *Ibid.*, p. 41.
[17] Quoted in A. B. Shah and C. R. M. Rao, *Tradition and Modernity in India* (Bombay, 1965), p. 117 f.

not necessarily be followed by an automatic or speedly disintegration of the caste system," and concludes that "instead, caste may continue to take on new functions and manifestations." [18] Kingsley Davis contends that "the increasing solidarity of castes over large geographical distances has led in some ways to a strengthening of the caste spirit, a spirit which has a new element in it: it is competitive." [19] And Selig Harrison in a study of politics in the state of Andhra in the years immediately after independence maintains that "caste has played so fundamental a role . . . that this examination becomes in effect a case history in the impact of caste on India's representative institutions." [20] Certainly, up to the present there is little to support the prevalent belief of many non-Indians that caste as a viable central factor in Indian life is doomed. On the contrary, in subtle and not so subtle ways it is asserting itself as a primary base for personal life and broader social action. Vividly apparent evils associated with caste are less evident; values of social cohesion and close personal relationships continue to be found in the ancient structure.

The situation is not quite the same in regard to the traditional joint family, wherein parents and their married sons with their wives and children live together in a common household. While the precise structure and size of such families has varied in different areas and among different caste or social groups, the role of the joint family in inculcating and continuing religious and social values and customs has been significant throughout much of Indian history. Today, while caste consciousness and the service of caste to its members can continue in a variety of ways, even when the static conditions of the past are replaced by increased mobility of living and occupation, it is not at all evident that the joint family can similarly adapt. Based as primarily they have been on geo-

[18] Oscar Lewis, *Village Life in Northern India* (New York, 1965), p. 83 f.
[19] *The Population of India and Pakistan* (Princeton, 1951), p. 175.
[20] Selig Harrison, "Caste and the Andhra Communists," *American Political Science Review*, 50 (July 1956), 379. Srinivas cites Harrison's study as "providing conclusive evidence of the decisive role played by caste in South India." *Caste in Modern India*, p. 26.

graphic propinquity and, frequently, cooperative family economic endeavor, such families are held by some observers "to be crumbling fast." [21] Other observers, while acknowledging that present economic and other factors are seriously affecting the joint family as traditionally conceived, maintain that the "tradition is so strong that it cannot die at once." [22] There is no doubt that it continues to be prevalent at many levels of Indian life. However, in many ways it appears to be the most vulnerable, and perhaps the least essential, of the traditional social structures.

The Purāṇic and Epic literature that has been central to Hinduism throughout the centuries continues today to fulfill its ancient functions. Royal patronage of drama, dance, and music based upon this literature may have ceased, but the support of the wealthy and of local village committees has combined with a renaissance of pride in Indian art forms to give the literature and its message a central place in Hindu-Indian life. Expositions of the Epics and Purāṇas, according to Professor V. Raghavan, "constitute one of the leading forms of popular religious instruction all over South India, especially in the Tamil country." [23] Professor Norvin Hein from his detailed study of the Rām Līlā, the dramatic pageant based upon the Epic Rāmāyaṇa which is presented yearly, especially throughout northern India, concludes that the pageant has been a "powerful influence" in North India and holds that in its modern form of the past three hundred years "it has carried traditional Hindu ideals to the youngest and simplest of many generations and has helped to preserve the continuity of Hindu culture in North India during periods of unusual stress and change." [24] Certainly all who have witnessed present-day Indian festivals, listened to Indian music, viewed Indian art and the dance, or at-

[21] C. D. Deshmukh in Shah and Rao, *Tradition and Modernity*.
[22] Sudhakar Chattopadhyaya, *Traditional Values in Indian Life* (New Delhi, 1961), p. 17.
[23] V. Raghavan, "Methods of Popular Religious Instruction in South India," in Haridas Bhattacharyya, ed., *The Cultural Heritage of India* (5 vols., Calcutta, 1956), IV, 505.
[24] Norvin Hein, "The Rām Līlā," in Singer, ed., *Traditional India: Structure and Change*, p. 94.

tended an Indian movie are aware that the literature and art of ancient and traditional Hindu India continues in modern form, frequently by the use of contemporary technology, to instruct the Hindu India of today.

Caste, the joint family, the sacred Epic, with their close associate, the cult, have been considered by many non-Hindus to be a residue that inevitably will be sloughed off as Hinduism seeks to be meaningful in the modern world. So, also, some Hindus have come close to this conclusion. The late Professor D. S. Sarma, a much-admired Hindu scholar in the liberal nineteenth-century and Gāndhīan tradition, said of the nineteenth- and twentieth-century renaissance of Hinduism:

the leaders of this renaissance, for the first time perhaps in the history of Hinduism, have been able to view their religion apart from the mythological, ritualistic and sociological forms in which it was embedded. . . . To many Hindus themselves, it was an eye-opener in this period to be taught that what really matters in religion is its philosophy based on spiritual experience, and not the particular social arrangements or the beliefs in particular deities in which it embodied itself in the past.[25]

But Sarma was speaking of "the leaders of the renaissance," and it is important to note that Indian and non-Indian forecasts of the disappearance of these traditional aspects of Hinduism come from those whose intellectual approach to religion frequently leads them to de-emphasize the roles of the intimate family social group and the cult in daily religious life. They are not aware of or they ignore reports like that of an Indian political scientist in 1961 who said that more Hindu temples had been built in the preceding ten years than in the previous two generations.[26] Religious and social pilgrimages to temples, great and small, continue to be an important part of Indian life, and are made easier through means of transportation identified with modernity. Ritualistic forms and mythological beliefs are no doubt threatened by modernity, but to expect their disappearance or radical alteration in the foreseeable future would

[25] D. S. Sarma, *Studies in the Renaissance of Hinduism* (Banaras, 1944), p. 637.
[26] Frank Thakurdas quoted in Shah and Rao, *Tradition and Modernity*, p. 186.

be to ignore the basic structure of life for the vast majority of the Hindu-Indian people.

The "modern" Hinduism proclaimed by groups such as the Rāmakrishna Mission, and evident in the welfare activity associated, for example, with the temple complex at Tirupatti in South India, does little to dispel the traditional myth and ritual of the masses. The educated Hindu may be determined to have a modern society and a secular state, and as a result do all he can to present a demythologized and less ritualistic Hinduism. Nevertheless, frequently the centers of this "new" Hinduism are also focal points for the expression of the traditional piety of the Hindu people. Some have rightly noted that in the instance of Tirupatti, where temple income is now used to support a university, hospitals, and so forth, the ancient religious center "has become the symbol and model of the new Hinduism" and represents for temple Hinduism "a religious reformation of a fundamental nature." [27] But there is no evidence that the meaningful Hindu myth upon which the temple complex rests and the cult that daily expresses itself at Tirupatti are less central in the minds of the devout pilgrims at the great temple. On the contrary, the "new" Hinduism there is revitalizing rather than de-emphasizing the myth and the worship it engenders.

Further, there is no question that karma, fate, astrology, and the conviction that deity will protect and aid you if you make the proper prayers, offerings, and vows continue to be at the very center of the religious beliefs of the masses of Hindu people. Dharma is equally central and is understood as that which is ethically right, as taught in the Epics and Purāṇas. It is these factors that not only encourage but require the cult that continues to be inherent in Hinduism. In company with so-called modern and educated members of other leading religions, the modern elite of Hinduism frequently criticize and disavow the beliefs and worship practices of the mass of their coreligionists. However, their position must not mistakenly be assumed to be a pattern for inevitable fu-

27 D. E. Smith, *India as a Secular State,* p. 251.

ture forms of Hindu cult, nor can the non-Hindu blithely identify his own ideas of proper cultic practice with that which may at some time emerge in Hinduism. As Professor Sarma himself admitted,

It is curious that the nation has gradually accepted almost all the items of the social reform programme that the Samājas stood for, but not their religious doctrines. The country is still faithful to the older religion with its lofty metaphysics, its ideal of renunciation, its wide toleration and the richness and variety of its popular worship. It prefers a spacious mansion of many rooms, though somewhat dusty and out of repair, to a neat, white-washed shed with up-to-date electric fittings.[28]

III

Professor Srinivas, whom we have quoted frequently, has written that "it could be said that on a short-term view Hinduism has been purified and strengthened by contact with the West." [29] If by "strengthened" it is meant that there is a heightened consciousness among educated Hindus that the essential philosophical-theological themes of Hinduism's great tradition are viable in the modern world; if it is implied that there is now an assurance and a pride where a few generations ago there was a feeling of inadequacy and humility in the face of the onslaught from the West; if it is suggested that Hinduism in the past century has found a voice enabling it to speak meaningfully to its own adherents and with confidence to others—if this is what is meant I doubt that many would disagree. If by "purified" Professor Srinivas is echoing Professor Sarma's separation of the great tradition of Hinduism from its "mythological, ritualistic and sociological forms" in the minds of the Hindu elite, remembering that this separation is in the *minds* of the elite and not always in their habits and actions, and certainly not in the minds, habits, or actions of the great mass of the Hindu people, then, again, the objective observer of contemporary Hinduism will tend to agree, despite the debate that will inevitably arise concerning the standards whereby "purity" is to be defined.

[28] Sarma, *Renaissance,* p. 147 f.
[29] Srinivas, *Caste in Modern India,* p. 160.

As we suggested earlier, today the continuing contact with the West is no longer one in which India and its various components are somewhat passive recipients. Rather, Indian society, culture, and religion are rapidly assuming, if they have not already attained, the status of partnership within a larger world enterprise. Within this new structure, to be modern is not only to import; it is also to participate in exchange that increases the value of the indigenous as well as incorporating into it previously foreign values now recognized as universal essentials for modern man, his society, and his spiritual quest.

Unexpected and disturbing questions requiring previously unimagined answers do pose dilemmas for traditional habits of thinking and behavior, though the dilemmas are frequently not evident to the masses within the tradition. However, when we consider what Hinduism has been and is for the Indian people, and what modernity is and possibly will be, there is little meaningful evidence that the ultimate decision of the Indian people will be one wherein the values of Hinduism will be discarded. For the Hindu man and woman of faith the dilemmas and the doubts they cause can be overcome by the rich teachings of the past that continue to be the strength of Hinduism today.

In the final words of Arjuna in the *Bhagavadgītā* as he addresses the incarnate Lord Kṛṣṇa:

Destroyed is my delusion and recognition has been gained by me through Thy grace, O Acyuta [Kṛṣṇa the Unfailing One]. I stand firm with my doubts dispelled. I shall act according to Thy word.[30]

Whatever may be the dilemmas confronting Hinduism in the latter half of the twentieth century, the promise it has given to the Indian peoples through the centuries continues unabated.

[30] *Bhagavadgītā*, XVIII.73, trans. by S. Radhakrishnan (New York, 1948), p. 381.

CHRONOLOGICAL CHART

Many dates in Indian history must be approximations. The following are given only as a broad guide to the general reader.

B.C. *circa* 1500–1200	Āryan migration into northern India.
1500– 900	Hymns of the *Ṛgveda*.
900– 500	Later Vedas; "priestly" or sacrificial religion (Brāhmanism).
700– 300	Major Upaniṣads.
600– 400	Beginnings of Jainism and Buddhism.
327– 325	Invasion by Alexander the Great.
300– 100 A.D.	Itihāsas: *Rāmāyaṇa, Mahābhārata* with the *Bhagavadgītā*.
A.D. 200 B.C.– 800 A.D.	Development of Purāṇas.
800	Śaṅkara.
1100	Rāmānuja.
1100	Beginnings of Muslim political power.
1250	Madhva.
1400–1600	The "Medieval Saints."
	Spread of popular Hinduism through work of Kabīr, Vallabha, Caitanya, etc.
1500	Beginnings of Sikhism.
1525–1700	Muslim Mughal Empire.

1750–1947	British rule of India.
1800–	Christian missions in India.
1830–1900	Beginnings of the contemporary renaissance of Hinduism; Ram Mohan Roy; Dayānand Saraswatī; Rāmakrishna, Vivekānanda, and others.

GLOSSARY

ācārya A spiritual guide, religious instructor.

advaita Nonduality. Identity of Brahman or the Paramātman, Supreme Soul, with the jīvātman or human soul.

Arjuna Warrior hero in the *Bhagavadgītā* (section of the *Mahābhārata*) who is instructed by the avatāra Kṛṣṇa.

Ārya Samāj "Society of Āryans." Religious society founded in 1875 by Dayānand Saraswatī that seeks to base Hinduism on the Vedas.

Āryan Peoples who invaded and settled in North India in the second millennium B.C. Identified with Vedas and Sanskrit culture.

āśram Hermitage, place of religious retreat.

āśrama Traditional four stages of life: brahmacārin or student, gṛhastha or householder; vānaprastha or hermit; and sannyāsin or homeless wanderer completely abandoning earthly ties.

Ātman The soul or self. Same as Brahman in Advaita thought. When distinguished from Brahman it is known as jīvātman, the individual soul.

avatāra Descent of a deity from heaven, thus an incarnation of God.

Bhagavadgītā "Song of the Adorable One." A portion of the Epic (Ithihāsa) *Mahābhārata,* in which the avatāra Kṛṣṇa reveals the Truth to the warrior Arjuna.

bhakti Attachment and devotion to a personal god.

bhakti mārga (yoga) Path of devotion to god. Mokṣa or liberation by adoration and faith.

Brahman The ultimate Divine, the Absolute Reality above all else.

Brāhman The priestly class. First of the four varṇas or traditional class and occupational groups.

Brāhmanism The "priestly" religion primarily associated with the Brāhmaṇas or liturgical cultic literature, *circa* 900–500 B.C. It has remained influential throughout Indian history.

Brahmo Samāj "Society of God." Founded in 1828 by Ram Mohan Roy with emphasis upon theism and reform.

Buddhism   Originally an Indian religion developing from teachings of Siddhārtha Gautama (566–486 B.C.), the Buddha. Later spread throughout Asia but almost disappeared in its Indian homeland.

caste   Indian "jāti," or an endogamous and, traditionally, occupational group. Not to be confused with the larger class structures, or varṇa, consisting of many jātis.

Dharma   Sacred or Divine Law: justice, righteousness, morality, religious obligation, etc. See ṛta.

dīkṣā   Religious rite; investiture of the sacred thread (upanayana); consecration; offering.

Dravidian   South Indian peoples; culture of pre-Āryan origin; linguistic group.

Dvaita   Taught by Madhva (13th century A.D.). Dualistic philosophy-theology. God, souls, and matter are eternally distinct.

guru   A teacher, spiritual guide and religious instructor.

Islam   Arabian religion centered around the Qur'an and the Prophet Muhammad. Entered Indian subcontinent *circa* 10th century A.D. Established ruling power in the North under varying dynasties culminating in the Mughal Empire of the 16th, 17th, and 18th centuries. Approximately one-ninth of the present Indian population is Muslim.

Itihāsa   Hindu Epics. Traditional legendary accounts of early heroic history. The *Rāmāyaṇa* and the *Mahābhārata*.

Jainism   Indian religion founded by Mahāvīra (599–527 B.C.) Rejected the Vedas and emphasized logic and experience.

jīvan-mukta   A free soul. A person who has attained freedom from karma and its limitations while still living physically.

jñāna   Knowledge. Noncognitive, intuitive knowledge of Brahman.

jñāna mārga (yoga)   Path or discipline of knowledge. Mokṣa or liberation by knowledge of identity of Brahman and Ātman.

joint family   Parents, married sons, and their families living together and, traditionally, engaged in a joint occupational endeavor.

Kabīr (1440–1518)   Religious teacher and reformer who emphasized common brotherhood of Hindus and Muslims.

karma   Work or action. All acts have their fruits or consequences and work together to create later conditions for the individual performing the acts.

karma mārga (yoga)   Path of service to god. Mokṣa or liberation by selfless action.

Kevalādvaita   Absolute nondualism. Identity of Brahman and Ātman taught by Śaṅkara (*circa* 800).

Kṛṣṇa (Krishna)   Popular god. Teacher in the Bhagavadgītā. Eighth avatāra of the great god Viṣṇu.

Laws of Manu   Ancient digest of laws, religious teaching, politics, and morality.

Lokh Sabhā   People's Assembly. Lower house of Indian Parliament.

Madhva Thirteenth-century philosopher-theologian. Taught Dvaita, i.e., God, souls, and matter are eternally distinct.

Mahābhārata The epic (Itihāsa) recounting the heroic legendary history and wars of the Bharata family. Contains the Bhagavadgītā.

mārga Path or way. In religion the path to release or mokṣa.

mokṣa (moksha) Liberation, release, from saṁsāra or the cycle of existence.

Oṃ Sacred syllable. "What has become, what is becoming, what will become—verily, all of this is the sound Oṃ." *Māṇḍūkya Upaniṣad,* verse I.

Paramātman The supreme Spirit, the Ultimate, Brahman.

pīr Muslim saint.

prakṛti Matter, as distinct from soul stuff or spirit (puruṣa).

Purāṇas Ancient Hindu mythologies relating the activities of the gods on earth.

puruṣa Spirit, soul, self, as distinct from matter (prakṛti).

Rāmānuja Eleventh-century philosopher-theologian who taught a qualified non-dualism (Viśiṣṭādvaita) wherein the world and the human self are real. Coming from Brahman, the human self, though dependent, has a continued individual existence. Rāmānuja emphasized devotion (bhakti) to God.

Rāmāyaṇa The epic (Ithāsa) recounting the heroic legendary adventures of Rāma, an avatāra of the great god Viṣṇu.

Rām Līlā Festival pageant depicting the activities of the Lord Rāma, as recounted in the Epic Rāmāyaṇa.

rites of passage Anthropological term indicating the ritual ceremonies accompanying the crisis events in human life, e.g., birth, puberty, marriage, death.

ṛṣi (rishi) Ancient sage. Those who heard (see śruti) the eternal Truth, the Vedas.

ṛta (rita) Divine law, the order of nature, proper, right in Vedic religion. See Dharma.

Śaivite (Śaivism) A worshipper of the great god Śiva.

saṁsāra The cycle of existence wherein all comes into being, flourishes, wanes away, and comes into being again.

saṁskāra Religious rite of purification and consecration.

Śaṅkara One of greatest philosopher-theologians of Hinduism, *circa* 800. Taught absolute nonduality. Brahman equals Ātman and Ātman equals Brahman.

sannyāsī A religious hermit or wanderer who has abandoned wordly attachments. The fourth āśrama.

Sanskrit Ancient sacred language of India in which the traditional "orthodox" religious literature was composed.

satī (suttee) The former practice in some groups of a widow's placing herself on her husband's funeral pyre.

Sikhism Indian religion founded by Nānak (1469–1538). Strictly monotheistic, incorporating aspects of both Hinduism and Islam.

Śivājī   South Indian King (1627–1680) hailed today for his leadership in founding a "Hindu" empire in resistance to the Muslim rule of the Mughals.

śruti   Something that is heard. The Vedas revealed to the ṛṣis.

śuddhi   Purification rite for Indians brought back into Hinduism primarily from Islam and, more recently, Christianity.

Śūdra   A member of any caste falling within the lowest of the four varṇa classifications. Not entitled to the initiation (upanayana) ceremony of the "twice-born."

Sūfī   A Muslim mystic.

swāmī   Literally, "Lord." A title used for religious teacher or spiritual preceptor.

Tantric   Type of Hinduism centering on mystical formulas, charms, and actions for the attainment of supernatural powers.

twice-born caste   Castes falling in upper three varṇa classifications, whose members, therefore, are entitled to the upanayana or sacred thread ceremony signifying rebirth.

upanayana   Initiation ceremony for the investitute of the sacred thread, signifying a "twice-born" status.

Upaniṣads   Philosophical-theological literature composed in first millennium B.C. that has served as the primary base for the later Hindu philosophies and metaphysical thought.

Vaiṣṇava (Vaiṣṇavism)   A worshipper of the great god Viṣṇu.

varṇa   Literally, "color." The four traditional classes of Indian society. Brāhman (priest), Kṣatriya (warrior, noble), Vaiśya (merchant, trader), and Śūdra (laborer).

Veda   Ancient, originally oral, literature (*circa* 1500–900 B.C.) containing the Ultimate Truth revealed to the ṛṣis.

Vedānta   Literally "end of the Vedas." Schools of Indian thought emphasizing the philosophical and metaphysical speculation of the Upaniṣads, especially the thought associated with Śaṅkara, Rāmānuja, and Madhva.

Viśiṣṭādvaita   Qualified nondualism wherein Brahman, man, and the world, while distinct from each other, form a unity, though the latter two are eternally dependent upon Brahman.

yoga   A methodological discipline of the body, mind, and soul or psyche having the goal of liberation from saṁsāra.

INDEX